SPORT ST▲CKING
The Resource Guide

By Jim Ross

ISBN: 978-0-945872-21-4

Great Activities Publishing C
PO Box 51158
Durham, NC 27717-115
(800) 927-0682
www.greatactivities.net

D1367776

FOREWORD

By Bob Fox

Founder & CEO of Speed Stacks, Inc.,
Founding Director of the World Sport Stacking Association

To have an accomplished and well-respected physical educator like Jim Ross undertake an entire book on sport stacking is both exciting and extremely gratifying. I've known Jim since introducing him to sport stacking in 2001. He's innovative, enthusiastic and seeks to find physical activities that reach and energize students of all ages and athletic abilities.

Speed Stacks began in 1998 with the vision of high-caliber, energetic PE professionals taking on a new, fun sport that promotes hand-eye coordination, dexterity, focus, fitness and activation of both sides of the body and brain. Because of teachers like Jim, sport stacking with Speed Stacks has grown at an exponential rate around the world in thousands of schools, youth organizations and at a highly competitive level governed by the World Sport Stacking Association (WSSA).

Speed Stacks, Inc. and the WSSA are grateful to Jim and his students at Orchard School for embracing sport stacking with such gusto. They have helped our vision become a reality. This book is a testament to the potential of what can be done when you combine a passion for kids and their athletic and academic skill development with a concept as simple as 12 plastic cups.

ACKNOWLEDGEMENTS & DEDICATION

This book would never have become a reality without the inspiration and support of the students at Orchard School. Many of the activities found in the following pages can be directly attributed to the enthusiasm, creativity and adventuresome spirit of the students I have enjoyed teaching over the past 23 years.

I would like to thank and acknowledge Speed Stacks, Inc. and the WSSA for developing the entire infrastructure for sport stacking. The genesis for many of the activities in this book comes from Speed Stacks, which truly is the leader in providing sport stacking equipment and resources to teachers around the world.

I would also like to thank the many colleagues and professionals who have inspired me during my travels around the state and the country. Thank you for allowing me to share!

This also includes my good friends, especially John Smith, Chip Candy, Tim Sabins, Gregg Montgomery, Don Puckett, Jim Rich, Melanie Champion, Nate Heath, Chris Benson, Marilena Canuto, Craig Mahler, Shawn Bennett, John Hichwa, Chris Morrill and the many others who have inspired, challenged, and otherwise helped transform my professional development.

Each of you have helped mold my thinking to what I believe Physical Education is and can be for our students today. To you I extend my whole-hearted gratefulness.

To my family - Theresa, Greg, and Brian. Thank you for your patience and unselfishness for allowing me to spend time away from home to share with others. My love to all.

Finally, a special thanks to Artie Kamiya and the Great Activities Publishing Company for giving me the chance to check off one of my "bucket list" items.

Life is, indeed, good.

JR

TABLE OF CONTENTS

WHAT IS SPORT STACKING?

Background: So what exactly is sport stacking? Quite simply, sport stacking is building and breaking down pyramids of specially-designed plastic cups, called "Speed Stacks," in specific patterns as quickly as possible. In this challenging activity, students must use both their left and right hands (and both sides of the brain as well) in recognizing patterns, sequencing their actions, and fixing mistakes all in the fastest time possible. Individuals looking to be active in sport stacking need no specialized skills or training.

Benefits: The important idea behind sport stacking is NOT what skills you'll need to participate, but rather what skills sport stacking helps to develop as a result of your participation! A person does not have to be athletic to participate successfully in sport stacking. For example, sport stacking may be performed on your own, against the clock (with a Speed Stacks StackMat or stopwatch), with a partner, or as part of a team. At our school, we have found sport stacking to be a type of activity that is enjoyed by students of all ages and ability levels! Most importantly, participating in sport stacking has real educational and personal benefits that include:

- Increasing fine motor coordination,
- Enhancing critical thinking skills,
- Helping to motivate and encourage non-athletically-inclined students,
- Increasing physical activity within your physical education classes,
- Increasing one's social and emotional confidence (or EQ "Emotional Intelligence"), and
- Creating a venue for using positive goal-setting skills for children and youth.

Join in the Fun! The sport of stacking cups is definitely on the rise! This book will provide teachers and parents with the necessary information for developing a sport stacking program at school, as an afterschool club, in a recreation setting, or at home. As outlined in the Table of Contents, this book has been designed to provide physical education teachers and others with a wide variety of activities, challenges, and integrated fitness games that can be used by individuals, in small groups and large classes. Fun variations to the basic patterns and activities are described in detail, along with great photos and illustrations to increase your enjoyment and student success! Finally, please be assured that all of the games and activities included in this one-of-a-kind resource have been "kid tested and kid approved!"

*Additional online resources are found at "speedstacks.com" and "thewssa.com."

CHAPTER ONE

GETTING TO KNOW YOUR PYRAMIDS

INTRODUCTION

Sport stacking involves three basic cup pyramids (3, 6, and 10 cups) and three basic stacking patterns (3-3-3, 3-6-3, and the Cycle). What follows is an abbreviated description of each. For complete details, I would encourage you to tap into all the great teaching resources provided by Speed Stacks, including a step-by-step instructional video, all found at www.speedstacks.com.

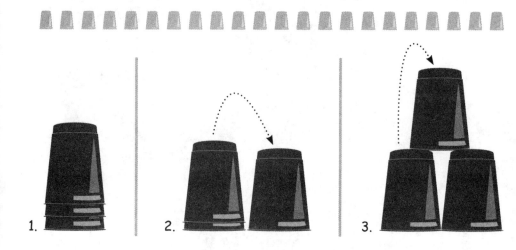

3 Cup Pyramid

1. Start with three cups in a single stack.
2. Using one hand, lift the top cup and place it to the side of the stack.
3. Use the opposite hand to lift the second cup and place it on top of the two cups.
4. To down stack, use the first hand to slide (and "pull") the top cup down onto the base cup that's on the same side as that hand.
5. Use the opposite hand to lift the single cup up and onto the other two cups.

6 Cup Pyramid
(The 3-2-1 Method)

1. Start with a stack of six cups.

2. Use one hand to lift three cups off the stack.

3. The opposite hand lifts two cups, leaving one cup as the base cup.

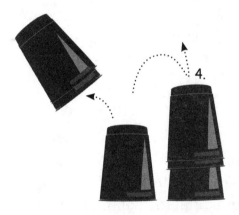

4. Beginning with the hand with three cups, release one cup, from the bottom, next to the base cup.

5. On the opposite side and with the opposite hand, release a second cup; this should create a base of three cups.

(continued next page)

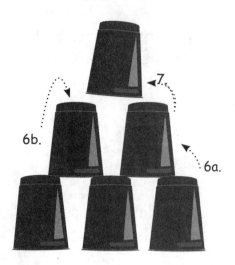

6. Alternating hands, (a) place one cup on top of and slightly off center of the base cup. (b) Add a second cup on the opposite side. This creates a second tier to the pyramid.

7. Finish up stacking by placing the last cup on top of the second tier.

8. To down stack, place one hand around the top cup and the opposite hand around the second tier cup on the same side as that hand. Pull the hands apart and down. The cups will slide together leaving three cups in one hand and two in the opposite hand.

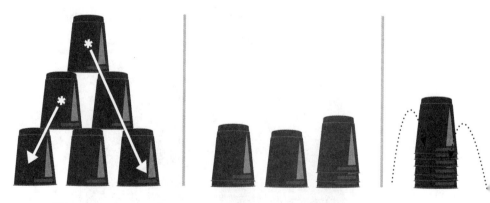

9. The down stack is complete when the cups are back to their original down stacked column of six cups.

10 Cup Pyramid

1. Begin with a stack of 10 cups.

2. (a) Slide five cups off the stack with one hand and (b) four cups with the opposite hand, leaving one base cup.

3. Build the first tier starting with the hand that has five cups and placing one cup to the side of the base cup.

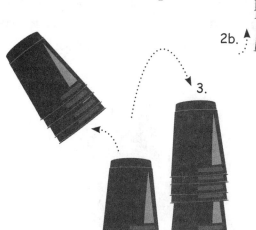

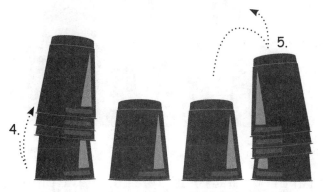

4. Using the opposite hand, place a cup on the opposite side of the base cup.

5. Place one more cup down from the first hand, creating a base of four cups for the first tier of the pyramid.

 (continued next page)

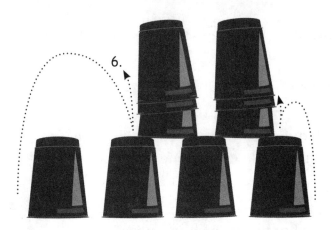

6. To start the second tier, place the first cup from the second hand **on top and in the middle of the first tier of cups**. Use alternating hands to place two more cups down.

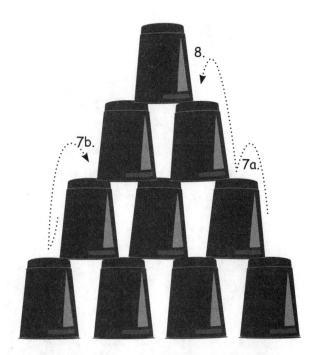

7. The third tier consists of two cups on top of the second tier.
8. Finish the up stack with one cup at the pinnacle.

9. To down stack, hold the top cup with the first hand and a third tier cup with the other hand. Pull the cups apart and down **diagonally**. This action will leave a stack in each hand (four in one and three in the other) and a separate 3 cup pyramid.

10. Lift the stacks in each hand and diagonally down stack the 3 cup pyramid. This will leave two stacks of cups (Six in one hand and four in the other). Finish by down stacking the cups into one column of 10.

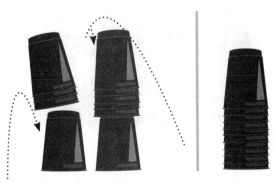

CHAPTER TWO

THE PATTERNS

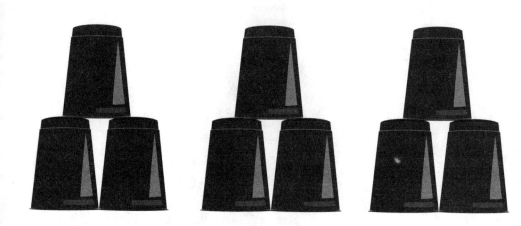

3-3-3

The 3-3-3 pattern starts with three separate stacks of three cups, in the down stack postion. Using alternating hands, the player builds a 3 cup pyramid from the first stack, followed by a second and third pyramid from the other two stacks. After completing the up stacking phase, the player returns to the first stack and begins the down stacking phase.

(3-3-3 Down stack)

3-6-3

The 3-6-3 pattern starts with three separate stacks, all in the down stack position: a 3 stack, a 6 stack and another 3 stack. Using alternating hands, the player builds a 3 cup pyramid from the first stack. From the second stack a 6 cup pyramid is built, followed by another 3 cup pyramid from the third stack. After completing the up stacking phase, the player returns to the first stack and begins the down stacking phase.

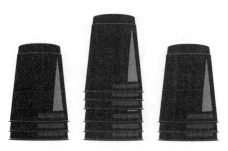

(3-6-3 Down stack)

6-6

The 6-6 pattern is part of the "Cycle" stacking pattern. It can also be used on its own in many of the games and activities. Starting with two stacks of six cups, build one 6 cup pyramid followed by a second 6 cup pyramid. After completing the up stacking phase, the player returns to the first stack and begins the down stacking phase.

(6-6 Down stack)

1-10-1

The 1-10-1 pattern is also part of the Cycle stack, and it too can be used on its own in many of the games and activities. The 1-10-1 pattern starts in a down stacked column of 12 cups. The top two cups are taken off, one cup in each hand, and placed on either side of the new column of 10. One cup must face up and one cup must face down (player's choice). Next, up stack the 10 as you learned on pages 11-12. Take up five cups in one hand and four cups in the other hand, leaving one cup (base cup) on the stacking surface. Starting with the hand that has five cups, place one cup down next to the base cup. Place a second cup down using the hand with four cups, followed by another cup from the five cup hand. This forms the bottom 4-cup layer of the 10 cup pyramid. Continue using alternate hands, but the first cup of the second level should be placed, by the second hand, on top and in the middle of the base layer. Continue building and alternating hands until the 10 cup pyramid is complete.

17

(continued next page)

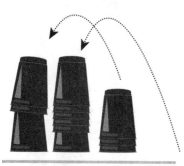

Note that down stacking a 1-10-1 pattern is different than down stacking a 10 stack on its own, as seen on page 13.

To begin down stacking the 1-10-1, pick up each single cup (the cups that are not part of the 10 cup pyramid). A reverse grip should be used on the cup that has the closed end down. This will put the cup in the correct position for down stacking the 10.

Position one cup over the top cup of the pyramid. The other cup is positioned over a cup on the third layer.

Using a diagonal and down motion, slide the cups in the same direction. The top cup should end up in a stack of five cups and the other cup should end up in a stack of four cups. There should be one 3 cup pyramid still standing.

Take all of the cups in the 5 stack and just one cup from the 4 stack and stack down the 3 cup pyramid as shown.

The result should be three stacks of cups: a 3 stack, 6 stack and another 3 stack.

The Cycle

The Cycle is a series of three patterns stacked in the following order. Remember to reference the Speed Stacks instructional materials to learn some important details about the Cycle, namely the transitions from one pattern to the next.

1. Begin with a 3-6-3 stacking pattern.
2. Down stack the 3-6-3.

3. Build a 6-6 pattern: Pick up and move the last 3 stack to the other and build a 6 cup pyramid. Build a second 6 cup pyramid using the 6 stack.
4. Down stack the two 6 cup pyramids finishing in a down stacked column of 12 cups.

5. Up stack and down stack a 1-10-1 pyramid.
6. Finish with the cups in a 3-6-3 down stack.

CHAPTER THREE

SPORT STACKING
GAMES & ACTIVITIES

INDIVIDUAL & PARTNER CHALLENGES

The following games and activities may be done alone but often are more enjoyable when done with a partner or in a small group. For every activity the player may be challenged in three different ways:

- Versus a clock (StackMat or stopwatch) for fastest time
- Versus a set time (for example: Can the pattern be completed in less than 20 seconds?)
- How many patterns can be completed in a set time?

The focus of each activity is to improve an individual's scores but may certainly be made into a competition between one or more additional players!

> **The following challenges require
> 1 Speed Stacks set per person,
> unless otherwise specified.**

Beat Your Best Score!

Equipment: 1 StackMat or stopwatch

Directions: After practicing the stacking patterns, it is time to test the speed! A partner and a stopwatch are needed for this activity. (If alone, it is best to have a StackMat to time the players. The StackMat has a built-in timer that is started and stopped by the player.)

Place both hands with the palms resting flat and lightly on the surface. On "go," begin a predetermined stacking pattern. The partner starts the stopwatch when the player's hands lift off the surface and stops the watch when the player taps the surface with both hands after completing the pattern. Record the time and switch roles. In the next round, try to beat the previous time. Remember to play by the rules! The person timing is also the judge!

Blindfolded Stacking

Equipment: 1 StackMat or stopwatch (optional)

Directions: This activity is best played after mastering any or all of the stacking patterns. Competitive stackers use this technique to fine-tune their stacking skills. Simply put, try any of the stacking patterns while blindfolded! A timer is optional but good to use just to see how fast each pattern can be completed. No peeking!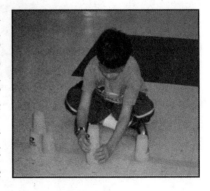

Partner Stacking

Equipment:
- 1 set of Speed Stacks per group
- 1 StackMat or stopwatch (optional)

Directions: What better way to practice something than with a partner? Well, this may prove to be a bit tricky. The patterns are the same for partner stacking as for individual stacking. However, now each player is responsible for half the stacking!

Stand side by side with a partner. Decide which stacking pattern will be completed. Put inside hands behind backs. That's right, the player on the right is the right hand and the player on the left is the left hand! The rules are the same as in individual stacking.

Each stack must be completed before players may move on to the next stack. To finish, each hand must be down on the playing surface at the same time! (If using a StackMat, the timer will not stop unless it is tapped with two hands at the same time!)

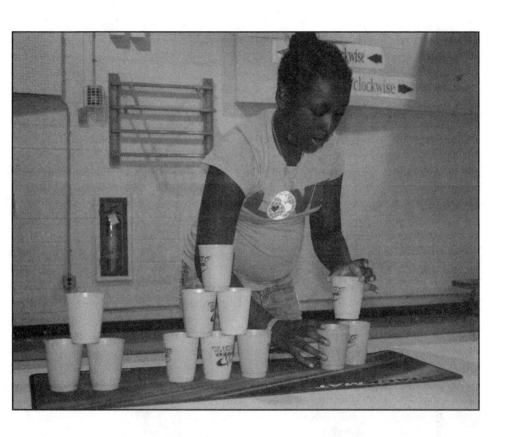

Upside Down Stacking

Directions: No, this is not stacking while being suspended upside down! For something completely different try any of the stacking patterns with the cups facing up! Set the cups up with the open end facing up. Complete the patterns in exactly the same way as regular stacking. This can be done with any of the patterns, alone, with a partner, or as a relay!

The Shuffle

Equipment:
- 12 cups (Six of one color and six of another color)

Directions: Two different colors (six cups of each color) are needed for this activity. Begin with the cups in a down stacked column of 12, six cups of one color atop six cups of another color. Pick up the top six cups with one hand and the next five cups with the opposite hand. Starting with the hand that has six cups, "shuffle" the cups one onto the other into a down stacked column of 12 (if done correctly the colors should alternate). Continue taking six and five cups in each hand (always start with the 6-cup hand). When the cups return to the original order, six of one color on top of six of the other color, the activity is finished. With no mistakes it should take 10 steps to complete the shuffle.

Shuffle start/end configuration.

Shuffle after first step.

Short Stack Shuffle

Equipment:
- 6 cups (Three of one color and three of another color)

Directions: This is actually a good training step before attempting "The Shuffle" (see previous). A player attempting the Short Stack Shuffle needs six cups, three cups of one color and three cups of another color. The cups start in a down stacked column of six, three cups of one color on top of the other color cups. The player takes the top three cups in one hand and the next two cups in the other hand, leaving one base cup. Starting with the hand that has three cups, the player alternates hands dropping cups, one at a time, back onto the base cup. If done correctly the colors will alternate in the stack. The player continues taking three cups and two cups in each hand and dropping the cups back onto the base cup. When the cups are back in the original position the shuffle is completed. Without any mistakes it should take five steps to complete the Short Stack Shuffle.

Note: Remind players to use the same hand to pick up the three cups each time. Also, players should always begin the "shuffle" with the same hand (the one with three cups).

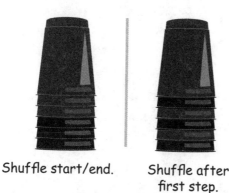

Shuffle start/end.　　Shuffle after first step.

Walking 3

Equipment:
- 3 cups per player
- StackMat or lines of tape

Directions: This activity requires three cups. Establish a start and finish line (no more than 3 feet apart). Place the cups in a down stacked position behind the starting line. On "go," up stack and down stack a series of 3 stacks. If alternating hands are used, the stack will "walk" forward. Keep stacking until the front edge of a cup touches the finish line. Finish in a down stacked postition. Be careful not to move cups forward illegally by accidental dragging or tipping. If a cup falls off, it must be returned to the previous position before moving forward again.

Note: Playing areas can be determined by using StackMats or by placing two lines of tape, approximately 3 feet apart, on a table or the floor.

Walking 3 Walkabout

Equipment:
- 3 cups per player
- StackMat or lines of tape

Directions: This is the extended version of the Walking 3. Tape or otherwise mark two lines 3 feet apart. One line is the start/finish line. Players may choose either line as the start/finish line. Place the cups in a down stack behind the starting line. On "go," up stack and down stack a series of 3 stacks. If alternating hands are used, the stack will "walk" forward. Keep stacking until the front edge of a cup touches the opposite line. Complete the down stack and then reverse directions. When one cup touches the start/finish line, finish in a down stack and stop the timer. Be careful not to move cups forward illegally by accidental dragging or tipping. If a cup falls off, it must be returned to the previous position before moving forward again.

Start/Finish and Turn Around Lines
(3' Apart)

Australian Walking 3

Equipment:
- 3 cups per player
- StackMat or lines of tape

Directions: This activity is performed exactly like the "Walking 3" (see previous) with one exception: the cups face open end up!

Establish a start and finish line (no more than 3 feet apart). Place the cups in a down stacked position behind the starting line. On "go," up stack and down stack a series of upside down 3 stacks. If alternating hands are used the stack will "walk" forward. Keep stacking until the front edge of a cup touches the finish line. Finish in a down stack. Be careful not to move cups forward illegally by accidental dragging or tipping. If a cup falls off, it must be returned to the previous position before moving forward again.

Start/Finish Lines
(3' Apart)

Walking A Thin Line

Equipment:
- 3 cups per player
- Tape (boundary lines)
- Balance beam or table
- 1 stopwatch (optional)

Directions: This activity takes "Walking 3" to new limits: performing stacking patterns on a balance beam! The trick is to perform a series of 3 stacks without the cups falling off the balance beam.

On the balance beam, create a starting line and a finish line about 3 feet apart (leave plenty of space at each end for the cups to fit). The player places the 3 cups behind the starting line in a down stacked position. On "go," the player begins, performing a series of 3 stacks. If the player correctly alternates hands while performing the stacks the cups will "walk" forward. The player continues stacking until the front edge of a cup touches the finish line. If a cup falls off the beam the player must stop and reposition the cups where the cup fell off. The player is finished when all cups are past the finish line in a down stack.

Note: A stopwatch may be used if players would like to see who is able to finish in a faster time.

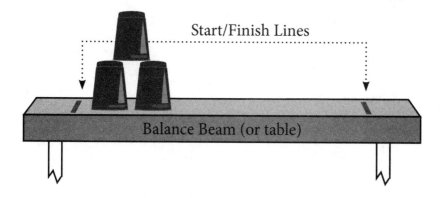

Start/Finish Lines

Balance Beam (or table)

End On Top

Equipment: 1 set of Speed Stacks per player (nine cups of one color and three cups of a different color)

Directions: This is a great activity to help players focus on performing the 3-3-3 and 3-6-3 patterns correctly and consistently. In the down stack position place a different color cup as the bottom cup on each 3 stack and the top cup on the 6 stack. The objective is to end up with the different colored cups on top of each stack at the end of the down stacking.

Flip Stacking

Equipment: 1 StackMat or stopwatch (optional)

Directions: This activity <u>does not</u> use one of the traditional stacking patterns. One set of cups is needed and a StackMat or stopwatch is optional.

Start with the cups in a down stacked column of 12. While alternating hands, build stacks of two cups by placing one cup down and another cup on top – closed end to closed end. When six stacks have been created, reverse and end up in a down stacked column of 12.

Closed Flip Stacking

Directions: Start with the cups in a down stacked column of 12. While alternating hands, build stacks of 2 cups by placing one cup with the open end up and another cup on top – open end to open end. When six stacks have been created, reverse and end up in a down stacked column of 12.

Alternate Flip Stacking

Directions: Start with the cups in a down stacked column of 12. Take one cup off the top and place down on the surface with the closed end down. Place another cup on top of the first (open end to open end). The second stack is completed just the opposite way with the first cup placed with the closed end up. The next cup is place on top – closed end to closed end. This continues, alternating stacks, until all 12 cups are used. The player is finished when the cups are returned to a down stacked column of 12.

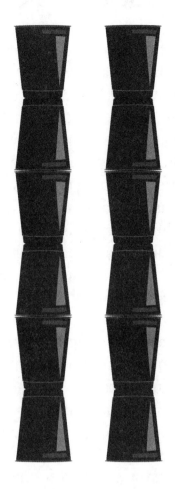

Twin Towers Flip Stacking

Directions: Start with a down stacked column of 12. Lift one cup off the stack and place on the surface. The second cup is placed on top of the first matching up end to end. Continue building until the tower is six cups high. Build a second tower. Down stack in reverse until the cups are back in a down stacked column of 12.

The Ultimate Tower

Directions: Beware! This activity requires a very steady hand to complete successfully! Start with the cups in a down stacked column of 12. Lift one cup off the stack and place it on the surface (best if the open end is down). The second cup is placed on top of the first, matching the ends of the cups. The third is placed on top of the second, again matching the ends. Building continues until all 12 cups are stacked creating one tower. Reverse the order back to a down stacked column of 12.

If the tower falls during building up, the player must stop and rebuild the fallen cups before continuing up. If the tower falls during the down stacking, the tower must be rebuilt with the fallen cups before continuing. Cups that have already been down stacked do not need to be rebuilt. This rule prevents players from simply knocking the tower over on the down stack.

3-3 Cross Stacking

Equipment: Six cups (three cups of one color and three cups of another color)

Directions: Set up two stacks of three cups in a down stack position, approximately shoulder-width apart. It is beneficial to have each stack a different color. Start by reaching with the right hand, retrieving a cup from the left stack and placing it down on the right side of the playing surface. Next, use the left hand to take a cup from the right stack and place that cup down on the left side. Continue to alternate right and left while building two 3 cup pyramids. When all the cups are in the "up" position, down stack the left pyramid with the right hand, followed immediately by down stacking the right pyramid with the left hand. The pattern is completed by reaching across with the right hand and bringing the left stack of cups back to the original position on the right side. Vice versa with the right stack of cups. When finished, the cups should be back in the original starting position.

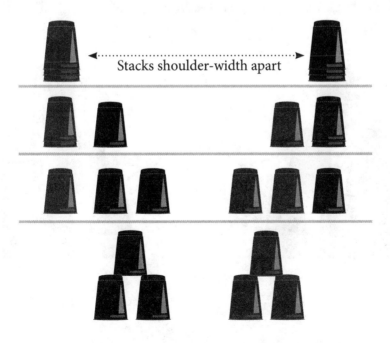

Stacks shoulder-width apart

6-6 Shuffle Cross Stack

Equipment: 12 cups (Six cups of one color and six cups of another color)

Directions: The player sets two stacks of 6 cups, each stack a different color, down on a flat surface. On the "go" signal, the player picks up both stacks at the same time. The player reaches across the body and places one cup from the right hand down on the left side of the playing surface, followed immediately by placing a cup from the left hand on the right side. The player continues to alternately place cups to each side until completing two 6 cup pyramids on opposite sides.

Starting Position

Finished Position

6-6 Shuffle Double Cross Stack

Equipment: 12 cups (Six cups of one color and six cups of another color)

Directions: The "double cross" continues the Shuffle Cross Stack until the cups are returned to the same down stacked position on the originating sides. For example, at the start if the 6 stack of orange cups are on the left and the blue stack is on the right, the double cross is complete when the stacks are back to the original starting position.

Starting Position

Finished Position

Zebra Stack

Equipment: 12 cups (Six cups of one color and six cups of another color)

Directions: This is a "crossing the midline" activity that requires focus and a light touch.

The starting position is two stacks of six cups, each stack being a different color. On the "go" signal, the player picks up both stacks, placing the first cup from each stack on opposites sides of the starting position. The next move is to place a cup from each stack on the original side, on top of the new base cup that should be the opposite color. The next move is crossing the midline to place a cup on each stack. The cups should be in new stacks of alternating colors. The player continues until the cups are once again in two stacks, each containing the same color cups and on the originating side of the playing area. Players are reminded to cross and uncross their arms when completing the stacking.

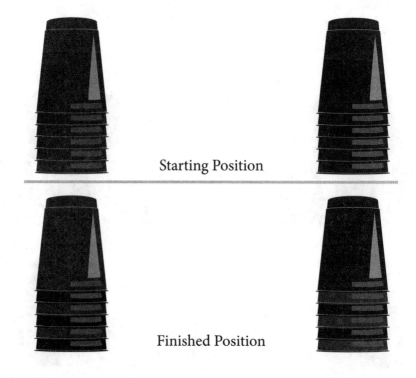

Starting Position

Finished Position

1-Legged Stacking

Equipment: 1 table for 2-4 students

Directions: Challenge the players to balance on one leg while performing stacking patterns. Along with learning and improving stacking patterns, players will be working on balance and developing core strength.

Suggested Patterns: 3-3-3, 3-6-3, 6-6, 1-10-1, or the Cycle.

Super Sport Stacking Challenge

Equipment: 1 StackMat or stopwatch per group

Directions: Players are given a set time for this activity. Simply put, the challenge is: How many completed stacking patterns can each player accomplish in 30 seconds? One player is the stacker while the other plays the role of judge and timer (if using a stopwatch). Try doing this for 1 minute. How about 2 minutes?

Suggested Patterns: 3-3-3, 3-6-3, 6-6, 1-10-1, or the Cycle.

Topsy-Turvy

Equipment:
- 1 set of Speed Stacks per group
- 1 spinning top (or plastic egg) per group

Directions: This is a good warm up activity for students to "loosen up" before being timed for the stacking patterns. Divide the players into 2's or 3's. Give each group a set of cups and a spinning top (a plastic egg also works in place of a top). One player starts as the "spinner." The spinner spins the top. His/her partner performs a stacking pattern for as long as the top spins. Switch roles.

Suggested Patterns: 3-3-3, 3-6-3, 6-6, 1-10-1, or the Cycle.

Scatter and Stack
(Christopher Walker, NC)

Equipment: 1 desk bell per group (optional)

Directions: A simple hand speed activity played with a desk bell, if available. The players sit facing one another with their cups in a down stacked column of 12. On the "go" signal, each player takes six cups in one hand and five cups in the other hand and places the cups in a scattered formation in front of them (open end down). When all the cups are scattered in front of them, each player restacks the cups into a down stacked column of 12. Players may not begin to restack until all the cups have left their hands. The fastest player to perform this rings the bell and wins the game.

1-2 Switcheroo

Equipment:
- 1 set of Speed Stacks per group
- 1 StackMat or stopwatch per group

Directions: Best described as a "speed drill," this activity is for two players (though three will work). A stacking pattern is selected by the teacher or by the players. Players stand one behind the other. The objective is to complete 25 stacking patterns in less than the time allowed.

Strategy Hint: The second player should stand just off the shoulder of the first player. As the first player starts the down stacking, the second player may move forward and have the hands close, but not touching the cups. When the first player completes the down stacking, the second player may start to up stack. The first player, having finished the pattern, should step back and then reposition as the second player starts the down stacking.

Suggested Patterns (& Times):
- 3-3-3 (<3 mins.)
- 3-6-3 (<4 mins.)
- 6-6 (<4 mins.)
- 1-10-1 (<5 mins.)
- The Cycle (<5 mins.)

Activity Shuffle

Equipment:
- 1 deck of playing cards per group
- 1 desk bell per group (optional)
- 1 StackMat per player (optional)

Directions: This is a two- or three-player game. The players sit facing each other with their cups, a bell, and deck of cards (face down) between them. Assign a task to three of the playing card suits. The SPADES are reserved for a designated stacking pattern.

For example:

HEARTS = dribble a ball with each hand
CLUBS = jogging laps
DIAMONDS = balance on 1 foot
SPADES= 3-3-3 stacking pattern

The number on the card determines the number of repetitions the players must perform the corresponding task. The game begins with one player flipping a card off the top of the deck. One card is turned over at a time, alternating between the players. As the card is turned over the players complete the activity and first one done rings the bell.

Note: Card values should be from 1-10. Eliminate the face cards or designate the value of a face card anywhere from 1 to 10.

Suggested Patterns: 3-3-3, 3-6-3, 6-6, 1-10-1, or the Cycle.

CREATE YOUR OWN PATTERN

Sometimes players just need to let go and do their own thing! Challenge the players to come up with a completely different stacking pattern. One rule: Each pattern must have a beginning position and an ending position. Encourage the students to be creative, perhaps changing the colors of the cups or using more than 12.

The Cohen Challenge

Directions: Marcus Cohen (a 5th grader) created a stacking challenge not with a twist but with a flip. As a player performs the up stacking part of a pattern, the player must flip and catch the cup before placing it upon the corresponding pyramid. Players must continue to alternate the hands when flipping and stacking. Players use the regular down stacking procedures.

Note: The easiest challenge is the 3-3-3. When trying the 3-6-3 Cohen Challenge, players must build the 6-cup pyramid one cup at a time rather than take three cups in one hand and two cups in the other hand (as would normally be done). The Cycle is the ultimate challenge.

The Lehman Cycle

Emeril Lehman (2nd grade) created a stacking pattern called "The Lehman Cycle." In order, the patterns are: 3-3-3-3, 6-3-3, 3-6-3, 1-10-1, 6-6 and ending in a 3-3-3-3 down stack position (the 3-3-3-3 is not performed a second time). Following is the procedure for "The Lehman Cycle":

1. Set the cups in a 3-3-3-3 down stack position.

2. Complete the 3-3-3-3 stacking pattern. When down stacking, use the first set of 3 cups to down stack the second set (creating a 6 stack). Continue down stacking the two other 3 cup pyramids. The player should end up in a 6-3-3 down stack position.

3. Perform a 6-3-3 stacking pattern. After completing the down stacking, move the last stack of cups (a 3 stack) to the opposite side. This will put the player in position to perform a 3-6-3 stacking pattern.

4. Perform the 3-6-3 stacking pattern. When down stacking, use the first stack (3 cups) to down stack the 6 cup pyramid. Use one hand to down stack the final 3 cup pyramid and place the cups on top of the other cups. This should create a single stack of 12 cups.

5. Perform the 1-10-1 stacking pattern. After using the single cups to start down stacking the 10 cup pyramid, each hand should have a stack of cups with a 3 cup pyramid remaining. Down stack the 3 cup pyramid using all the cups in each hand. This will leave the cups in a 6-6 down stack position.

6. Complete the 6-6 pattern, ending in a 3-3-3-3 down stack position.

HEAD TO HEAD

The following games and activities are designed as 1 vs. 1 competitions, though more players may be added. Unless otherwise written, any and all stacking patterns may be used to play each of the games and activities. In all cases, the patterns used should be decided on before the game is started!

Ring My Bell

Equipment:
- 1 desk bell per group
- 1 StackMat per player(optional)

Directions: Players face each other with their sets in front. A desk bell is positioned between the players and their sets. The group decides on which stacking pattern to perform. On a "go" signal, the players try to be the first to complete the pattern, up stacking and down stacking. When done, the first player to ring the bell wins!

Flipping Out

Equipment:
- 1 desk bell per group
- 1 deck of playing cards per group
- 1 StackMat per player (optional)

Directions: Players face one another with their sets of cups in front. Each group has a pack of playing cards; it is not necessary for each group to have all 52 cards. After deciding on the stacking pattern, one player flips the top card. The number on the card indicates the number of times the stacking pattern must be performed. First one to finish and ring the bell wins!

For example:

Pattern to be played is 3-3-3. The card that is flipped is a 4. The first player to perform the 3-3-3 (up stacking and down stacking) four times, wins!

Diamonds In The Rough

Equipment:
- 1 deck of playing cards per group
- 1 desk bell per group (optional)
- 1 StackMat per player (optional)

Directions: Players face one another with their sets of cups in front. In addition to the set of cups per person, each group is given a deck of cards and a desk bell. The desk bell and deck of cards are placed between the players. The group decides which stacking pattern will be performed. The players take turns flipping over the top card of the deck. When a "diamond" is turned over, the players immediately begin performing the chosen stacking pattern for as many times as the card indicates (i.e. a 2 of diamonds would mean to perform the pattern two times). The first player to complete the task rings the bell and wins that round. Players start the next round by picking a stacking pattern and flipping the top card over.

Hearts Are Wild!

Equipment:
- 1 deck of playing cards per group
- 1 desk bell per group (optional)
- 1 StackMat per player (optional)

Directions: Players face one another with their sets of cups in front. Give each group a pile of playing cards containing a mix of all suits.

Assign a pattern to a specific suit (clubs = 3-3-3, diamonds = 3-6-3, spades= Cycle, hearts = choice). One player flips the top card. The first player to perform the assigned pattern and rings the bell wins! If a heart is flipped over, the player who turned the card chooses the pattern!

Tic-Tac-Toe

Equipment: 1 tic-tac-toe board with X/O markers
               1 StackMat per player (optional)

Directions: Players sit at opposite ends of the playing area. A tic-tac-toe game board and pieces are placed halfway between the players. Players pick a stacking pattern to perform. On a "go" signal, the players complete the stacking pattern. When finished, the players run to the middle and place a game piece on the board. Once the piece is down it may not be moved. Players run back and complete the stacking pattern again. Play continues until there is a win or a tie. Start a new game.

All Patterns Tic-Tac-Toe

Equipment: 1 tic-tac-toe board with X/O markers
1 StackMat per player (optional)

Directions: Players sit at opposite ends of the playing area. A tic-tac-toe game board and pieces are placed halfway between the players. On a "go" signal, the players stack the cups up and then down using the 3-3-3 pattern. When finished, the players run to the middle and place a game piece on the board. Once the piece is down it may not be moved. Players run back and complete the 3-6-3 pattern. The next time back, players complete the Cycle pattern. This is followed by the 3-3-3 pattern once again. Play continues until there is a win or a tie. Start a new game.

Tic-Tac-Toe with Defense!

Equipment: 1 tic-tac-toe board with X/O markers
1 StackMat per player (optional)

Directions: Players sit at opposite ends of the playing area. A tic-tac-toe game board and pieces are placed halfway between the players. Players pick a stacking pattern to perform. On a "go" signal, the players stack their cups up and down. When finished, the student runs to the middle. The player has a choice of putting one of his/her pieces on the board OR taking one of his/her opponent's pieces OFF the board! Once a piece is moved, the player may not change his/her mind. Players run back and complete the stacking pattern again. Play continues until there is a win or a tie. Start a new game.

(continued next page)

TIC-TAC-TOE

X	X	X	X	X
O	O	O	O	O

Score Four

Equipment: 1 "Score Four" game board with markers
 1 StackMat per player (optional)

Directions: This game is similar to Tic-Tac-Toe. The object is to be first to align four playing pieces in a row (horizontally, vertically or diagonally). Playing partners sit at opposite ends of the playing area. A Score Four game board and pieces are placed halfway between the players. Players pick a stacking pattern to perform. On a "go" signal, the players stack their cups up and down. When finished, the player runs to the middle. The player places one piece on the board and then returns to stack again. With each return trip comes a new strategy – do you go for four in a row or do you block your opponent?

(continued next page)

SCORE FOUR

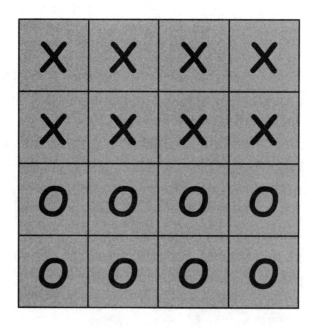

Zip Line

Equipment:
- 1 set of Speed Stacks per group
- 1 die per group
- 1 StackMat or stopwatch per group
- 1 center cone

Directions: Assign stacking areas around the perimeter of the room. In the middle of the playing area place a tall cone (or some other large object). Divide the class into 2s or 3s, giving each group a set of cups, a StackMat (or stopwatch) and a die. Stacking patterns may be directed by the teacher or student selected.

To start the game, a player within each group rolls the die. The number that appears on the die is the number of "zips" a player must complete in the fastest time possible. A "zip" is completed when the player completes the stacking pattern, runs to touch the center cone and then returns to the stacking area. The timer is started when the player begins the first pattern and is stopped after the player returns from touching the cone (or after the designated number of zips are completed).

After each player is done, the times are compared. The next round starts when a new pattern (or the same) is selected and the die is rolled.

I Can Do That Stack!

Directions: The ultimate head to head competition! Players create their own stacking patterns. There must be a starting formation with all of the cups in a down stack position and there must be an ending position with the cups, again, in a down stack position. In between, just about anything goes! Once a student has a pattern, s/he may challenge another player to master his/her pattern! Of course, the player must teach his/her pattern first. Afterwards, the players can go head to head to see who can complete the pattern the fastest!

Fox and Hound

Equipment:
- 4-8 sets of Speed Stacks per group
- 4-8 StackMats per group (optional)
- 1-2 tables (optional)

Directions: This game is best played with one or two tables connected end to end, but may also be played on the floor. Though played 1 vs. 1, the class should be divided into groups of 3-4 because of the amount of space and equipment involved.

Establish a playing area on tables (as diagramed below) or by placing 4-8 sets of cups in an oval/circle on the floor. The distance depends on the space allowed, but the playing area should be at least 10 feet in length.

One player is designated as the "fox" and picks one station at which to start. The other player is the "hound" and must begin at the station opposite the fox. The players select a stacking pattern to be performed and in which direction they will be moving (clockwise or counter clockwise). When ready, the fox and hound begin performing the selected stacking pattern. After completing the pattern, the players move to the next station. The objective is for the hound to catch the fox by completing the patterns faster. If the hound is able to stand behind the fox while the fox is completing a pattern, the hound wins. If the fox is able to make it back to the first station before being caught by the hound, then the fox wins.

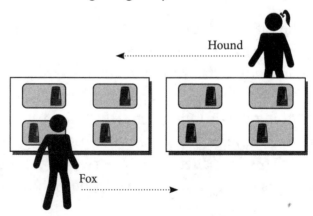

Lucky Clover

Equipment:
- 1 deck of playing cards per group
- 1 desk bell per group (optional)
- 1 StackMat per player (optional)

Directions: This is a 2- or 3-player game. The players sit facing each other with their cups, a bell, and deck of cards (face down) between them. The players begin flipping cards off the top of the deck. One is turned over at a time, alternating between the players. When a club ("lucky clover") is turned over, the players begin performing the selected stacking pattern. The number on the card dictates how many stacks (stacking patterns) a player must perform in order to complete the task. The first player to complete the task rings the bell and is given all of the flipped over cards. The players return to flipping the cards one at a time until another "clover" shows up and the stacking begins again. Play continues until all of the cards have been flipped over. The player with the most cards wins the game.

Note: Card values should be from 1-10. Eliminate the face cards or designate the value of each worth up to 10.

Suggested Patterns: 3-3-3, 3-6-3, 6-6, 1-10-1, or the Cycle.

Challenge Roll

Equipment:
- 1 die per group
- 1 desk bell per group (optional)
- 1 StackMat per player (optional)

Directions: This is a 1 vs. 1 game that is good to practice any of the stacking patterns. Split the class into groups of 2 (groups of 3 will work also). Every player should have a set of cups. Give each group a bell and a die. Players set up facing each other with the bell placed between the two.

One of the players sets the challenge by calling out a stacking pattern to perform. After the pattern is selected, the die is rolled. The number that ends up on the die dictates the number of times each player must perform the selected pattern. The players place both hands flat on the ground to start. One player yells "go," and the game begins. Each time the pattern is performed, the player calls out the number. When the correct number of patterns are performed, the player rings the bell (optional, simply calling out "DONE!" works also).

Players select the same or a new pattern, roll the die and start another game.

Suggested Patterns: 3-3-3, 3-6-3, 6-6, 1-10-1, or the Cycle.

Activity Shuffle Challenge

Equipment:
- 1 deck of playing cards per group
- 1 desk bell per group (optional)

Directions: This is a 2- or 3-player game. The players sit facing each other with their cups, a bell, and deck of cards (face down) between them. Assign a task to 3 of the playing card suits. The SPADES are reserved for a designated stacking pattern.

For example:

- HEARTS = dribble a ball with each hand
- CLUBS = jogging laps
- DIAMONDS = balance on 1 foot
- SPADES= 3-3-3 stacking pattern

The number on the card determines the number of repetitions the players must perform the corresponding task. The game begins with one player flipping a card off the top of the deck. One card is turned over at a time, alternating between the players. As the card is turned over, the players complete the activity. The first player to complete the task receives 1 point. After 5 minutes, the player with the most points wins the game. If time allows, players start a new game with new partners.

Suggested Patterns: 3-3-3, 3-6-3, 6-6, 1-10-1, or the Cycle.

Notes: Card values should be from 1-10. Eliminate the face cards or designate the value of a face card anywhere from 1 to 10.

SMALL GROUPS

The games and activities in this section are for groups of 4-10 players, though more players may be added. Generally, the players compete against the other members within their group. However, in some activities groups may compete against other groups.

Four Square

Equipment:

- 4 sets of Speed Stacks per group
- 4 StackMats per group (optional)
- Tape (boundaries)

Directions: This is played similar to the traditional four square. The playing area consists of a larger square (8'x8') divided into four smaller squares (4'x4'). One square is designated as the "Champion Square". A second square, adjacent to the Champion Square, is designated as the Entry Square. To start the game, one player sits in each square with a set of cups. Extra players line up at the entry square. The player in the entry square calls out a pattern to perform such as the 3-3-3. On the "go" signal, all four players perform the stacking pattern. The last player to finish is out. The extra players are the referees and help determine who was last. Players all rotate one square toward the champion square. The player in the champion square does not move (unless s/he is last in completing the pattern; in that case s/he is out). The player in the Champion Square receives a point for every round s/he survives. If a player receives 3 points in a row, s/he is declared a Grand Champion and goes to the end of the line (no monarchies here!).

Suggestion: If a player performs a pattern incorrectly, as judged by the referees, s/he is out. There may be more than one player out after any given round.

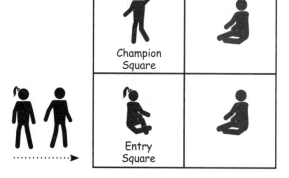

Ring My Bell Relay

Equipment:
- 1 set of Speed Stacks per group
- 1 desk bell per group
- Tennis balls or markers (optional)

Directions: Split the class into smaller groups of 2-4 students. Assign each group a spot behind a starting line. Place a set of cups on the floor approximately 15 feet away. Further away (15 feet), place a bell. On the "go" signal, the first player from each line runs to the middle and performs a pre-determined stacking pattern. After completing the pattern, the player continues forward and rings the bell. This signals the next player to go. The first player returns to the starting line. Teams have 3 minutes to record as many "dings" of the bell as possible. The teacher sets the winning total.

Suggestion: To help keep track of each team's score, have them pick up a marker or tennis ball after ringing the bell. The group counts the number of collected markers at the end of the time limit for a score.

Super Sport Stacking

Equipment:
- 1 StackMat or stopwatch per group
- 1 table (Note: 4 groups can fit on one table)

Directions: This is a great activity to practice specific stacking patterns. Players can do this with a partner, but may find this to be more enjoyable with a small group of classmates. The group picks one pattern to complete. Each player has 1 minute to complete the stacking pattern as many times as possible. When ready, the first player begins stacking the cups in the selected pattern. At the end of the time limit, the next player tries to beat the score of the first player.

The time limit may be lengthened or shortened depending on the ability level of the players.

Suggested Patterns: 3-3-3, 3-6-3, 6-6, 1-10-1 or the Cycle.

50 Stacks

Equipment:
- 1 StackMat or stopwatch per group
- 1 table (Note: 4 groups can fit on one table)

Directions: This activity is done in a relay format. Each group of 3-5 players is given a set of cups and a StackMat or stopwatch. When ready, one player starts the timer and begins a stacking pattern. When finished down stacking, the next player performs the same stacking pattern. Players within the group take turns performing the stacking pattern, making sure to count the number of stacking patterns completed. When 50 stacks (stacking patterns) have been completed, the timer is stopped and the time is recorded. Scores may be compared against other group scores or start a second round and try to beat the group score!

Note: Increase the number with the shorter stacks and decrease the number with the longer stacks.

Suggested Patterns: 3 stack, 6 stack, 3-3-3, 3-6-3, 6-6, 1-10-1 or Cycle.

Luck Of The Draw

Equipment:
- 1 set of Speed Stacks per group
- 1 StackMat per group (optional)
- 1 deck of cards per group
- Tables (optional)

Directions: Run in relay format, this activity is performed in groups of 2-4. Give each group a set of cups and a deck of cards. Designate a spot on the floor or at a table for each group to perform their stacking pattern. The deck of cards should be placed, face down, somewhere near the stacking area. Each group line is positioned 3-5 feet behind the stacking area.

On the "go" signal, the first player in each line runs to the stacking area and performs a designated stacking pattern. Upon completion of the pattern, the player flips one card over and then runs back to the line, giving a high 5 to the next player in line. The players continue to alternate turns, trying to complete as many stacking patterns (and flipping as many cards) as possible within the 3-minute time limit.

When time is up, the groups collect the cards they turned over. Each group counts the cards to determine their scores. A sample of the point system is listed below:

Card	Point Value	Card	Point Value
Ace	10	Eight	80
Two	20	Nine	90
Three	30	Ten	100
Four	40	Jack	- 10
Five	50	Queen	- 10
Six	60	King	25
Seven	70	Joker	100

Table Stack

Equipment:
- 4 sets of Speed Stacks per player/group
- 1-4 StackMats or 1 stopwatch per table (optional)
- 1 table per player/group

Directions: Set up four sets of cups - one in each quadrant of the table. It doesn't matter which set the first player starts at, but everyone performs the same stacking patterns. On the "go" signal, the first player starts the stacking pattern at the first set of cups. S/he then moves to the next set and so on. The player is finished when s/he either stops the timer or taps the table in front of the first stack. It is best if a timer is used (StackMat with a timer or a stopwatch). If no timer is available, have the players go head to head at different tables, using a bell (or the tapping of the table) to indicate when each player is finished.

Progressive Cycle Stack

Equipment:
- 4 sets of Speed Stacks per player/group
- 1-4 StackMats or 1 stopwatch per table (optional)
- 1 table per player/group

Directions: This activity is designed to reinforce each segment of the Cycle stacking pattern. Set up four spots around the table. At one spot set 12 cups in the 3-6-3 down stack position. At the second spot set two stacks of 6. The third spot should have a down stacked column of 12. Finally in the fourth spot another set of 12 cups in a 3-6-3 down stack position. On the "go" signal, the first stacker starts the timer (StackMat or stopwatch), completes a 3-6-3 stacking pattern and then moves on to the two stacks of 6 where s/he completes a 6-6 pattern. At the third spot, the player completes a 1-10-1 stacking pattern. Finally, at the fourth spot, the player completes the Cycle pattern. The timer is stopped after the completion of the Cycle.

Progressive Pattern Stack

Equipment:
- 4 sets of Speed Stacks per player/group
- 1-4 StackMats or 1 stopwatch per table (optional)
- 1 table per player/group

Directions: Set up four spots with cups in each of the following down stack positions: 3-3-3, 3-6-3, 6-6 and 3-6-3. On the "go" signal, the player starts the timer and completes the 3-3-3 stacking pattern. S/he moves to the next spot and completes the 3-6-3 pattern. Moving to the third spot, the player completes a 6-6 pattern. Finally the player moves to the fourth spot and competes the Cycle stacking pattern. The timer is stopped after the Cycle is complete.

Table Sprint Stack

Equipment:
- 4 sets of Speed Stacks per player/group
- 1-4 StackMats or 1 stopwatch per table (optional)
- 1 table per player/group

Directions: Players in this game receive practice performing the three competition stacks under timed conditions. Set up four stations on a table with cups in the following down stack positions: 3-3-3, 3-6-3, 3-6-3, and 3-3-3. On the "go" signal, the player starts the timer and completes the 3-3-3 stacking pattern. S/he moves to the next spot and completes the 3-6-3 pattern. Moving to the third spot, the player completes a Cycle pattern. The player finishes at the fourth station, completing a 3-3-3 stacking pattern. The timer stops following the completion of the final 3-3-3 pattern.

Walking 3 Relay

Equipment:

- 3 cups per group
- 1 StackMat or stopwatch per group

Directions: Small groups can participate in the Walking 3 Relay - competing against time or other groups. Using the "Walking 3" technique described previously (see page 26), each player takes a turn "walking" his/her cups the length of the mat. Player 1 starts the StackMat or stopwatch and begins the Walking 3. Player 2 takes over when player 1 reaches the opposite end of the playing area. Player 2 must walk the cups back to the start. This continues until all players on each team have had a chance to "walk" the cups. The last player stops the timer.

Go Fish

Equipment:
- 1 set of Speed Stacks per player
- 1 StackMat per player (optional)
- 1 set of stacking pattern index cards per group

Directions: This activity is designed for groups of 2-4. On 3"x5" index cards, write down different stacking patterns (one per card). Each group has its own set of cards. A set of cards should consist of a minimum of five cards for each stacking pattern. If fewer patterns are being used, more copies of the patterns should be prepared.

All the cards are face down and scattered where the group is playing. The game begins with one player picking a card and turning it over. Starting at the same time, the players perform the stacking pattern indicated on the card. When the stacking pattern is completed, the first player to complete the pattern has a choice between taking the card or taking another player's card! If the player chooses to take an opponent's card (hopefully to make a match), the leftover card is put back, face down, into the scattered pile.

The objective is to collect as many pairs of cards as possible within the time limit. If a player collects two cards of similar stacking patterns, s/he turns both cards over. The turned over cards are a match and may not be taken by another player. At the end of 3 minutes, the player with the most matches wins!

Leap Frog

Equipment:
- 1 set of Speed Stacks per player
- 1 StackMat or stopwatch per group
- 1 cone per group

Directions: Split the class into smaller groups of 2-3. This can be played with the entire class at the same time, but is best if each group has its own timer. Create a playing area by designating a start/finish line at one end and a "turn around" line at the opposite end. Place a cone on the "turn around" line for each group.

Each group picks a pattern to perform (NOTE: if doing this as a class activity, all the groups should do the same pattern). When the group is ready the timer is started (i.e. StackMat or stopwatch). While holding a set of cups, the first player in line takes three jumps (2 feet to 2 feet) forward, places the cups on the ground and begins performing the stacking pattern. As soon as the first player begins stacking, the second player (with his/her own set of cups) begins to jump forward. When the second player reaches the first player, s/he takes three more jumps past the first player. After the third jump past the first player, the second player begins the stacking pattern. The next player (with his/her own set of cups) may not start jumping until the player in front finishes jumping and begins stacking. This continues the length of the playing area and back, with each group traveling around a cone. The timer stops when the last player jumps past the start/finish line.

Lucky Doubles

Equipment:
- 1 set of Speed Stacks per group
- 1 sheet of paper per group
- 1 set of dice per group
- 1 pencil per group

Directions: This is a game best suited for 3-4 players. Give each group a pencil, a sheet of paper, a set of dice and a set of cups (each player may have his/her own set also). Before starting the game, the group makes a space on the paper for each player. The group must also decide on the stacking pattern to be performed. A time limit of 5-10 minutes is set.

Play begins with a roll of the dice. Each player takes his/her turn rolling the dice until "doubles" (each die showing the same number) are rolled. The player rolling the "doubles" begins performing the stacking pattern. The stacking player scores a point for every completed stacking pattern. Stacking continues until another "doubles" is rolled. At this point, the new player, having just rolled the "doubles", begins performing the stacking pattern. The player having just finished records his/her score on the score sheet. The player scoring the most points within the set time limit wins the game.

First Century

Equipment:
- 1 set of Speed Stacks per group
- 1 sheet of paper per group
- 1 set of dice per group
- 1 pencil per group

Directions: This is a game best suited for 3-4 players. Give each group a pencil, a sheet of paper, a set of dice and a set of cups (each player may have his/her own set also). Before starting the game, the group makes a space on the paper for each player. The group must also decide on the stacking pattern to be performed. The players' goal is to be the first to score 100 points!

Play begins with a roll of the dice. Each player takes his/her turn rolling the dice until "doubles" (each die showing the same number) are rolled. The player rolling the "doubles" begins performing the stacking pattern. The stacking player scores a point for every completed stacking pattern. Stacking continues until another "doubles" is rolled. At this point, the new player, having just rolled the "doubles", begins performing the stacking pattern. The player having just finished records his/her score on the score sheet. The first player to reach 100 stacks (points) wins the game.

LARGE GROUPS

These games and activities are for class-size groups or larger! Unless otherwise specified, provide one set of Speed Stacks per player.

Stack Attack!

Equipment: 1 hoop per player

Directions: Split the class into two or more groups. Divide the playing area in half so each group has a "home" area (for more teams divide the playing area so each group has their own area). Within each "home" area, have each player place a hoop on the floor. Inside the hoop, each player up stacks his/her cups (decide on the 3-3-3 or 3-6-3). On the "go" signal, all the players go to another group's home area and down stack one set of cups. They bring the cups back to their own home areas and up stack the cups again. At the end of a 2-minute time limit, the group with the most up stacked sets wins.

Extinction

Directions: Divide the group into four or more teams. Set up a large playing area with stacking stations at one end or around the outside of the playing area. The game starts as a tag game. The object is to tag players on other teams. If tagged, a player must go to the stacking area and perform a stacking pattern (determined by the teacher). Once the stacking pattern is completed the player may return to the game. However, if all players on a team are in the stacking area, that team is eliminated (or becomes extinct) from the game and must continue stacking until the game is completed. The game is over when all the teams but one are eliminated.

Note: Any stacking pattern will work in this game. For the shorter patterns (i.e. 3-3-3), designate a number of stacking patterns that must be completed before rejoining the game (i.e. five 3-3-3 stacks must be completed).

Success/Try Again

Directions: Divide the playing area in half, designating one side as the "success" side and the other as "try again." Assign players to each half, each with a set of cups. Pick out a pattern for the players to perform (3-3-3 or 3-6-3 works best). The players are scattered on each side of the playing area. Each player challenges someone on his/her side to a contest to see who is the fastest stacker. No one may turn down a challenge. If a player wins on the success side, s/he stays and challenges someone else on the success side. If a player loses on the success side, s/he moves to the try again side and challenges someone. Players starting on the try again side do just the opposite - winners move to the success side, losers stay and challenge someone on the try again side.

Peaks and Valleys

Directions: Divide the class into two groups: mountain goats and antelopes. Give each player a set of 12 cups and scatter the players around the playing area. After each player finds a spot, mountain goats, who live in very hilly terrain, make an up stacked 3-6-3. The antelopes (living in the valleys) leave their cups in a down stacked column of 12. On a "go" signal, the players travel to other cups and either up stack (mountain goats) or down stack to a column of 12 (antelopes).

Note: The cups are not moved to another location. After 1-2 minutes, the team with the most cups wins. Switch roles and play again. Other stacking patterns may also be used.

King/Queen Of The Hill

Directions: Make a series of stations around the room, one station for every two players. Place two sets of cups at each station along with two StackMats if you have them. Assign the players evenly to each station. Designate one station as the #1 station or "top of the hill." Select a stacking pattern for the entire class to perform. On a "go" signal, the players compete, 1 vs. 1, at each station. The winner moves up one station toward the top of the hill. The losing player moves down a station toward the bottom. If a player wins at the top of the hill, s/he stays at the top. Begin another round. The rounds are quick. Once the players understand which direction to move, the game moves quickly.

Chicken Dance Stacking

Equipment:
- Music player
- Song: "The Chicken Dance"

Directions: This is a great activity for creating repetition of a pattern in a fun and distracting kind of way! Any version of the song "The Chicken Dance" may be used. Begin playing the song. During the verses of the song, the players start stacking a pattern. It is best if the pattern used is one of the more simple patterns such as the 3-3-3. During the chorus, the players stop stacking and must perform the chicken dance. When the verse begins again, the players return to stacking as fast as possible. This is also a great activity for a family fun night!

Actions for chorus of "The Chicken Dance":
- Make "chicken beaks" with the hand open and close four times with the beat. "Peeping" sounds are allowed!
- Make wings by tucking hands under the armpits and flap four times with the beat
- Wiggle downwards for four beats.
- Stand and clap four times with the beat.

Suggested Patterns: 3-3-3, 6 stack, 3-6-3, 6-6.

<u>SHUTTLES & RELAYS</u>

Shuttles and relays can be fun and lively if the groups are kept small to limit any waiting for the players. Teams can be run against one another (one winner) or against a clock (StackMat or stopwatch). When running against a clock, give the groups a score or goal that must be accomplished before time runs out. Competing against a clock also allows for practice opportunities.

Note: Unless otherwise indicated, any of the stacking patterns may be used for the relays.

3 Person Shuttle

Equipment:
- 2 sets of Speed Stacks per group
- 2 StackMats per group (optional)
- 2 tables per group (optional)

Directions: Divide the class into groups of 3. Set up the playing area, placing one set of cups on the end of each table. Position the tables approximately 10-15 feet apart (tables are optional, this may also be run on the floor).

This activity is timed for 3-5 minutes with all groups starting and ending at the same time. On "go," the first player in the line of two, stacks a pre-determined pattern. Upon completion, this player runs to the other table and gives the player a high 5. This player, after receiving the high 5, completes the stacking pattern. When finished, the player runs back to the opposite line and high 5s the next player. This continues until the time limit expires. The group counts the number of stacks completed.

Note: Markers may be used to help keep track of the number of completed stacking patterns.

3 Person Skill Shuttle

Equipment:
- 2 sets of Speed Stacks per group
- 2 StackMats per group (optional)
- 1 basketball per group
- 2 tables per group (optional)

Directions: Divide the class into groups of 3. Give each group a basketball. Set up the playing area, placing one set of cups on the end of each table. Position the tables approximately 10-15 feet apart (tables are optional, this activity may also be run on the floor).

Set the timer for 3-5 minutes. Groups start and end at the same time. On "go," the first player in the line of two stacks a pre-determined pattern. Upon completion this player dribbles the basketball to the other line and hands the ball to the player. This player, after receiving the ball, completes the stacking pattern. When finished, the player dribbles back to the opposite line and hands the ball to the next player. This continues until the time limit expires. The group counts the number of stacks completed. (Markers may be used to help keep track of the number of completed stacking patterns.)

Other Skills to Add:
- Running with a football.
- Overhand throw (follow the pass).
- Dribbling a soccer ball with the foot.
- Passing a ball with the foot (follow the pass).
- Basketball chest, bounce, or overhead pass (follow the pass).

3 Person Fitness Shuttle

Equipment:
- 2 sets of Speed Stacks per group
- 2 StackMats per group (optional)
- 1 basketball per group
- 2 tables per group (optional)

Directions: Divide the class into groups of 3. Set up the playing area, placing one set of cups on the end of each table. Position the tables approximately 10-15 feet apart (tables are optional, this activity may also be run on the floor). Set the timer for 3-5 minutes. All groups start and end at the same time. On "go," the first player in line (two-player line) performs a designated exercise. The player then completes a pre-determined pattern. Upon completion, the player runs to the other line and high 5s the next player. This player, after receiving a high 5, completes the exercise followed by the stacking pattern. When finished, the player runs back to the opposite line and high 5s the next player. This continues until the time limit expires. The groups keep count of the number of stacks completed. (Markers may be used to help keep track of the number of completed stacking patterns.)

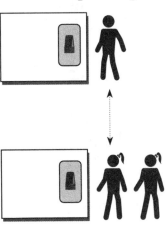

Note: Exercises may be changed by calling out, or place cards at the tables with a list of written exercises. Players would perform the exercises in order.

Some Suggested Exercises:
- Any Jump Rope Skill (with or without a rope)
- Push Ups
- Curl Ups
- Bounce Overs (add a 6-inch hurdle to each group)

Stacking Pattern Relay

Equipment: 3 sets of Speed Stacks per group

Directions: Place three sets of cups in the playing area in front of each group. Space the sets approximately 10 feet apart. Specify which stacking pattern will be used and set up the cups in a down stack position accordingly. On "go," the first player runs out and completes the stacking pattern. S/he performs the same stacking pattern at each set of cups before returning to the line and high fiving the next player in line who goes. First team to finish wins.

Note: If running against a clock, have the players count the number of stacks performed (counting in 3's). Challenge the groups to complete a specific number of stacks in the time allowed.

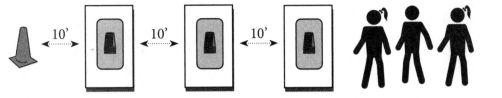

Up and Down Relay

Equipment:
- 3 sets of Speed Stacks per group
- 1 cone per group
- 3 tables per group (optional)

Directions: Position the teams of 2-4 players at one end of the playing area. In front of each team place three sets of cups. Each set should be 10 feet apart. Place a cone at the opposite end of the playing area. On "go," the first player in each line up stacks a 3-6-3 at the first set of cups. The player leaves the cups in an up stacked position and then moves on to the second and third sets, leaving each set in an up stacked 3-6-3. After completing the third set, the player continues and tags the cone at the end of the playing area and then returns to the line, giving the next player a high 5. The second player runs out and down stacks the three sets in order, tags the cone at the end and returns to give the next player in line a high 5. The relay continues until all players have performed two (three, four, or five) times.

Note: If running against a clock, have the players count the number of up stacks and down stacks performed (counting in 3's). Challenge the groups to complete a specific number in the time allowed.

10'-15'

Distance Relays

Equipment:
- 1 set of Speed Stacks per group
- 1 table (Note: 4 groups can fit on one 6 foot by 30 inch table)
- 1 StackMat or stopwatch per group

Directions: Four-player relay races are a fun and important part of sport stacking competition. For details of official relay competition, visit The World Sport Stacking Association at www. thewssa.com. The official tournament distance for team relays is 7 feet from the starting line to the edge of the table. For this relay, move the table 10-15 feet away. The first player starts at the stack (not behind the starting line). The first player starts the clock and begins a stacking pattern. Upon completion, s/he runs back to the line and high 5's the next player in line. The second player completes the stacking pattern and returns. The group continues until each player has performed the stacking pattern <u>four</u> times! When the last player has stacked four times, s/he stops the timer. Compare times with other groups, set a time for all groups to beat, or challenge each group to beat their own time!

Three Jump Stack Relay

Equipment:

- 1 set of Speed Stacks per group
- 1 cone per group
- 1 stopwatch for the class

Directions: Divide the class into groups of 2-3. Position all of the groups behind a designated starting line. At the opposite end of the playing area, place cones in a straight line. The distance between the starting line and the line of cones is determined by the amount of the playing area available and the grade level of the class (a longer distance for higher grades). Set a timer for 3 minutes.

Rules:

- On the "go" signal, the first student in each group makes three jumps forward (2 feet to 2 feet) while holding onto a set of cups.
- At the end of the third jump, the player places the cups on the floor and performs the pre-selected stacking pattern.
- After completing the stacking pattern, the player takes three more jumps (taking the cups with them), stopping after the third jump to complete the stacking pattern once again.
- When the player crosses the line of cones (this could be done on the first, second or third jump), s/he completes the stacking pattern one more time and then runs back to his/her partner.
- The next player may go after receiving the cups from the player returning from the playing area.
- A group "wins" if every player in the group is able to complete the task under the time limit.

Owl Hop Stack Relay

Equipment:
- 3 sets of Speed Stacks per group
- 1 cone per group

Background: This relay has a multicultural thread as it is based

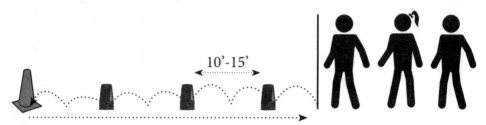

upon an Inuit (Eskimo) game called the Owl Hop. To perform the owl hop, a player hooks one foot behind the knee and bends down. The player then hops (jumps on one foot) forward.

Directions: Set your class in a standard relay format with 2-4 players in each group. Place three stations of cups equal distances away from each other (10-15 feet apart) for each group. Designate one end of the playing area as the start/finish where the groups are located. At the opposite end of the playing area, place a cone for each group.

On the "go" signal, the first player from each group performs the "owl hop" to the first set of cups. Once there, s/he begins performing the stacking pattern. When completed, the player performs the "owl hop" to the next set of cups and begins the stacking pattern. After finishing the third stacking pattern, the player hops to the cone, tags the cone and runs back to the line. The second player begins after receiving a high 5 from the first player.

The three sets of cups in the relay may all be the same pattern (all patterns work) or may be a combination of any or all of the patterns.

This relay may also be run against a designated time limit (possible multiple winners) or in a traditional race format.

Grizzly Bear Stack Relay

Equipment:
- 3 sets of Speed Stacks per group
- 1 cone per group

Background: Another traditional type of relay, the Grizzly Bear Stack Relay also helps to develop upper body strength. The "grizzly bear" walk is performed by traveling on the hands and feet.

Directions: Set your class in a standard relay format with 2-4 players in each group. Place three stations of cups equal distance away from each other (10-15 feet apart) for each group. Designate one end of the playing area as the start/finish where the groups are located. At the opposite end of the playing area, place a cone for each group.

On the "go" signal, the first player from each group performs the "grizzly bear" walk to the first set of cups. Once there, s/he begins performing the stacking pattern. When completed, the player performs the "grizzly bear" walk to the next set of cups and begins the stacking pattern. After finishing the third stacking pattern, the player performs the "grizzly bear" walk to the cone, tags the cone and runs back to the line. The second player begins after receiving a high 5 from the first player.

The three sets of cups in the relay may all be the same pattern (all patterns work) or may be a combination of any or all of the patterns.

This relay may also be run against a designated time limit (possible multiple winners) or in a traditional race format.

Speed Boat Stack Relay

Equipment:
- 3 sets of Speed Stacks per group
- 1 scooter per group
- 1 cone per group

Background: If scooter boards are available for use, this relay supports the development of the stacking patterns while working on upper body strength. In place of the running, players kneel on the scooter boards and use their hands to propel themselves toward the cup stations.

Directions: Set your class in a standard relay format with 2-4 players in each group. Place three stations of cups equal distance from each other (10-15 feet apart) for each group. Designate one end of the playing area as the start/finish where the groups are located. At the opposite end of the playing area, place a cone for each group.

On the "go" signal, the first player from each group travels aboard the scooter to the first set of cups. Once there, s/he begins performing the stacking pattern. The player remains on the scooter board while stacking. If the player falls off, s/he stops stacking until s/he is back on the scooter. When completed, the player performs the "scoots" to the next set of cups and begins the stacking pattern. After finishing the third stacking pattern, the player scoots to the cone, tags the cone, picks up the scooter and runs back to the line. The second player begins after receiving the scooter from the first player.

The three sets of cups in the relay may all be the same pattern (all patterns work) or may be a combination of any or all of the patterns. This relay may also be run against the clock or against teams.

Sport Stacking Biathlon

Equipment:
- 1 set of Speed Stacks per station
- 1 table per station (optional)
- 1 StackMat or stopwatch per station
- 3 cones

Background: This activity can be run with teams or as an individual event. It combines running and stacking much like a traditional biathlon combines cross country skiing with rifle shooting. Participants compete against each other, as well as acting as judges/timers. The biathlon is a race divided into five stages with the fastest time winning the race.

Playing Area: Establish a running track within the playing area. The track may be any length. Most likely the track length will be determined by what the playing area allows. Set up stacking stations inside or outside the running track. It is helpful to have a StackMat at each station, although stopwatches will also work. Place three cones inside the track. Below is a set up for a class size of 20-60 students.

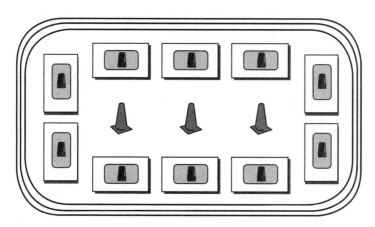

Set Up: Assign each student to a station. The stations should have tables, StackMats and cups. The tables should have a minimum of two students per table: one player and one judge.

 (continued next page)

The Event: On the "go" signal, players start their timers (StackMats or stopwatches held by judges) and begin performing a 3-3-3 stacking pattern. The player must <u>correctly</u> complete the pattern <u>four times</u> before leaving the table. After completing the stacking patterns, each player runs a lap around the track, returning to the same table. DO NOT stop the timer. This is the first stage. For each stage the stacking pattern changes:

Stage 1 = 3-3-3
Stage 2 = 3-6-3
Stage 3 = 6-6
Stage 4 = 1-10-1
Stage 5 = Cycle

When a player finishes all five stages, ending with a fifth running lap, s/he stops the timer. Places are determined by the recorded times.

Event Suggestions:
- Give the judges a red or green card to let the players know if the pattern was completed correctly (green) or incorrectly (red).
- Write the pattern names on cards. Have the judges place the card on the table to help remind the players which pattern is to be performed.

Penalties: If a player completes a stacking pattern incorrectly, s/he must run and tag the closest middle cone as a penalty and then perform the pattern again.

Variations:
- Use only one stacking pattern, especially for beginners.
- Increase the distance run during each stage by having the players run two laps instead of one lap.
- Increase the number of laps to be completed during each stage: first stage = one lap, second stage = two laps, etc.

Stacking Pentathlon

Equipment:
- 1 set of Speed Stacks per station
- 1 table per station (optional)
- 1 StackMat or stopwatch per station
- 1 basketball per station
- 1 soccer ball per station
- 1 jump rope per station
- 1 tennis ball per station

Background: The pentathlon is a five-event contest which has its origins in the Ancient Olympic Games. In the Ancient Pentathlon, Olympic athletes competed in the long jump, javelin throw, discus, a short running event called the "stadion," and wrestling. The Modern Pentathlon is also comprised of five events but the skills selected are considered to be what would be required of a late 19th century soldier: shooting, fencing, swimming, equestrian and cross country running.

In this version, players will alternate between sport stacking and performing specific sport skills.

Playing Area: Establish a running track within the playing area. The track may be any length and most likely will be determined by what the playing area allows. Set up stacking stations inside or outside the running track. It is helpful to have a StackMat at each station, although stopwatches will also work. Below is a set up for a class size of 24-60 students.

(continued next page)

Set Up: Assign each player to a station. The stations should have tables, StackMats and cups. In addition to the stacking equipment, supply a basketball, soccer ball, jump rope and throwing ball (such as tennis ball or foam ball) at each station. The tables should have a minimum of two students per table: one player and one judge.

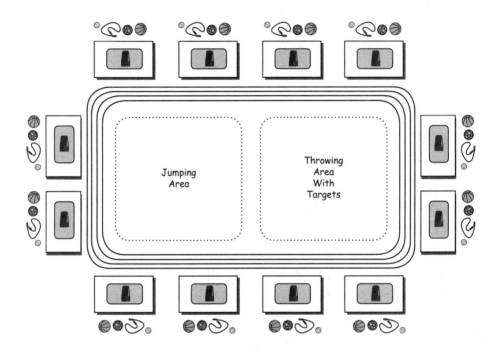

The Event: On the "go" signal, players start their timers (StackMats or stopwatches held by judges) and begin performing a designated stacking pattern. The player must correctly complete the pattern three times before leaving the table. After completing the stacking patterns, each player completes a skill challenge. DO NOT stop the timer. For each stage, the stacking pattern AND the skill changes.

When a player finishes all five stages, ending with the fifth stage skill, s/he stops the timer. Places are determined by the recorded times.

Stages:

Stage 1 = Pattern: 3-3-3   Skill: Jog 1 lap
Stage 2 = Pattern: 3-6-3   Skill: Dribble basketball 1 lap
Stage 3 = Pattern: 6-6   Skill: Dribble soccer ball 1 lap
Stage 4 = Pattern: 1-10-1   Skill: Jump rope 50 times
Stage 5 = Pattern: Cycle   Skill: Throw to target

Penalties: Players must correctly perform each stacking pattern three times before leaving the table for the skill portion of each stage.

Event Suggestions:

- Give the judges a red or green card to let the players know if the pattern was completed correctly (green) or incorrectly (red).
- Write the names of the patterns and skills to be performed on cards. Have one card for each stage. The judges place the cards on the table to help remind the players which pattern and skill are to be performed.

Variations:

- Use only one stacking pattern, especially for beginners.
- Perform skills associated with only one sport (i.e. basketball: dribbling, wall passing, lay ups, spot shooting, defensive slides).
- Change the type of skills the players must perform away from the table.

Locomotor Stacking Pentathlon

Equipment:

- 1 set of Speed Stacks per station
- 1 table per station (optional)
- 1 StackMat or stopwatch per station

Background: The pentathlon is a five-event contest which has its origins in the Ancient Olympic Games. In the Ancient Pentathlon, Olympic athletes competed in the long jump, javelin throw, discus, a short running event called the "stadion", and wrestling. The Modern Pentathlon is also comprised of five events but the skills selected are considered to be what would be required of a late 19th century soldier: shooting, fencing, swimming, equestrian and cross country running.

During this event, players will perform different stacking patterns interspersed with performing different locomotor skills. This is an excellent opportunity to assess locomotor skill achievement.

Playing Area: Establish a running track within the playing area. The track may be any length and most likely will be determined by what the playing area allows. Set up stacking stations inside or outside the running track. It is helpful to have a StackMat at each station though stopwatches will also work. Below is a set up for a class size of 20-60 students.

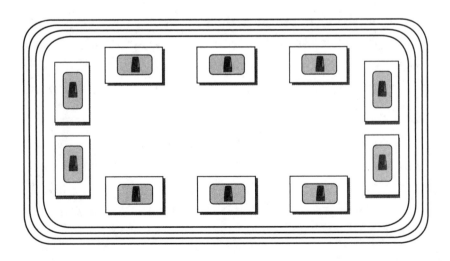

Set Up: Assign each player to a station. The stations should have tables, StackMats and cups. The tables should have a minimum of two students per table: one player and one judge.

The Event: On the "go" signal, players start their timers (StackMats or stopwatches held by judges) and begin performing a designated stacking pattern. The player must <u>correctly</u> complete the pattern three times before leaving the table. After completing the stacking patterns, each player completes a locomotor skill challenge. DO NOT stop the timer. For each stage, the stacking pattern AND the locomotor skill changes:

Stages

Stage 1 = Pattern: 3-3-3	Skill: Jog 1 lap
Stage 2 = Pattern: 3-6-3	Skill: Skip 1 lap
Stage 3 = Pattern: 6-6	Skill: Gallop 1 lap
Stage 4 = Pattern: 1-10-1	Skill: Slide step 1 lap
Stage 5 = Pattern: Cycle	Skill: Grapevine step 1 lap

When a player finishes all five stages, ending with the fifth stage skill, s/he stops the timer. Places are determined by the recorded times, fastest time being the best.

Penalties: Players must correctly perform each stacking pattern three times before leaving the table for the locomotor skill portion of each stage.

Event Suggestions:
- Give the judges a red or green card to let the players know if the pattern was completed correctly (green) or incorrectly (red).
- Write the names of the patterns and locomotor skills to be performed on cards. Have one card for each stage. The judges place the cards on the table to help remind the players which pattern and locomotor skill are to be performed.

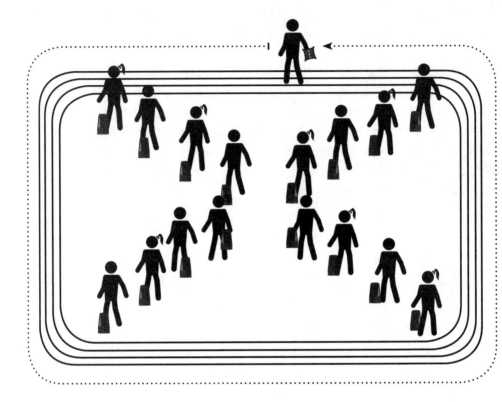

Short Track Stack

Equipment:
- Speed Stacks sets (as needed)
- Spot markers (optional)
- 1-2 bean bags

Background: The inspiration for this activity came after watching short track speed skating during the Winter Olympics. The activity can run up to 10 minutes with breaks and changes in direction.

Directions: Divide the group into four lines, setting up like spokes on a wheel. One player stands on the outside with a bean bag. The outside player travels around the other players, finally placing the bean bag at the head of one of the lines. The players in that line perform a pre-selected stacking pattern. When completed, the players race around the other groups and try to make it back to a space in their line. Meanwhile, the outside player takes the place of one of the runners. When the group makes it back to the line, one player is left out and becomes the new outside player. Once the players understand the game, add another outside player/bean bag to get more groups up and running.

Note:
- All players should run in one direction (clockwise or counterclockwise).
- Reinforce with the players to run around the other groups and not between them.
- If there are more players, create more lines or create more games. The lines are best if the numbers are kept to 4-6 in a line.
- Uneven numbers? Designate two players to drop the bean bag on the outside. This can be done taking turns (using one bean bag) or at the same time (using two bean bags).

Suggested Patterns: 3 stack, 6 stack, 3-3-3, 3-6-3, 6-6, 1-10-1, Cycle.

Fishing Derby

Equipment:
- 1 set of Speed Stacks per group
- index cards with stacking patterns per group

Directions: Write the names of different stacking patterns on 3"x5" index cards – one pattern per card. The more cards available for the game, the better. Divide the class into smaller groups of 3-4. Assign each group a "home" area around the perimeter of the playing area. The home area is where the stacking will be performed. This area may be at a table or on the floor. In the middle of the playing area scatter the index cards face down. This is the "fishing hole" with the cards representing fish.

On the "go" signal, the first person from each group runs to the middle of the playing area and picks up one card. The players bring the cards back to their groups. The player retrieving the card stacks first. After everyone in the group has performed the stacking pattern, a second player retrieves a new card from the "middle."

The groups have 5 minutes to "catch" as many fish as possible! All stacking patterns may be used with Fishing Derby!

Island Hop

Equipment:
- 3 sets of Speed Stacks per station
- 1 scooter per group
- Index cards with stacking patterns per group

Directions: This activity combines sport stacking with traveling on scooter boards. Split the class into groups of 2-3. Designate a "home base" for each group around the playing area. Give each group a scooter board. Create "islands" around the playing area by placing sets of cups around the playing area in a scattered formation. At each "island" place a card indicating which stacking pattern is to be performed at the island. In addition, at least three sets of cups should be at each "island" so more than one player is able to visit.

Set a time limit of 5 minutes (this may be shorter or longer). On the "go" signal, the first player from each group travels to an island while sitting on his/her scooter. After completing the pattern, the player returns home. The second player must travel to a new island. The objective is for the groups to travel to as many islands as possible in the time allowed. If all of the islands have been visited, the players may return to previously visited islands as time allows.

Note: It may help players to identify different islands by color-coding the islands. This may be accomplished by using different colored cups (the same color at each island) or cones to help identify the islands.

Stacking the Himalayas

Equipment:
- 13 sets of Speed Stacks (13 stations)
- 1 pack of playing cards per group
- Index cards with stacking patterns
- Cone or polyspot (optional)

Background: Located in Asia, the Himalaya Range is the highest mountain range in the world with over 100 mountains exceeding 7,200 feet in height.

Directions: Create the "mountain peaks" of the Himalaya Range by scattering sets of cups around the playing area. Number each "mountain" from 1 to 13 (or use "J," "Q" and "K" for the Jack, Queen and King instead of "11," "12" and "13"). Place an index card at each set of cups indicating the stacking pattern to perform with the available cups.

Divide the class into groups of 2-3. Give each group a deck of cards. Assign each group to a "home base" somewhere around the perimeter of the playing area (a cone or poly spot will help players remember where their "home base" is located).

Set a 5-minute time limit for the activity. On "go," each group flips over one card. The number (or letter) showing indicates which "mountain" the players travel to during their turn. For example, if an "8" is overturned, the player would run to "Mountain 8" and perform the indicated stacking pattern. After stacking, the player returns to home base and the next card is overturned. The next player runs to the mountain, performs the stacking pattern and returns. The objective is to travel to as many mountains as possible as time allows.

Variations: Rather than having the players run, change the locomotor pattern or use scooters to reach each "mountain."

Team Stack-Athlon

Equipment:
- 1 set of Speed Stacks per 2 groups
- 1 StackMat or stopwatch per 2 groups
- 1 table per 2 groups (optional)

Directions: This activity is played with groups of 5. Each player within a group is assigned one stacking pattern to perform. The teacher or the group can decide on the assignments. Two groups are assigned to a table or StackMat. While one group is performing, the other group acts as referees and scorers. Each player has three attempts to complete the assigned pattern correctly. The times for each attempt are recorded on a score sheet. After the team has completed the time sheet, the total of the best times is recorded. Scores are compared to all other group scores to determine the "Stack-athlon Champion" of the day!

PATTERN	PLAYER	Time 1	Time 2	Time 3	Best Time
3-3-3					
3-6-3					
6-6					
1-10-1					
Cycle					
			Total Time		

Note: This activity can be played once each class to determine a "daily champion" or it can be run as a round-robin tournament with groups competing against multiple groups within a class period(s).

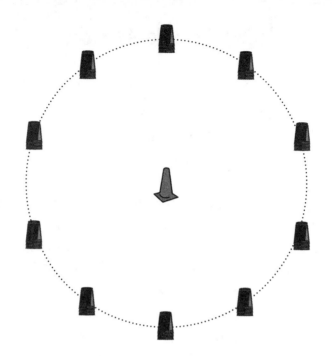

Zippity-Doo-Daa!

Equipment:
- 1 set of Speed Stacks per group
- 1 cone

Directions: Divide the class into groups of 2-3. Station the groups around the perimeter of the playing area. Give each group one set of cups. In the middle of the playing area place a large cone (something the players can tag with their hands). Select one pattern the class will perform.

On "go," one player from each group performs the stacking pattern. After completing the pattern, the player runs and tags the cone in the middle of the playing area before returning to high 5 his/her partner (the next player). The group scores 1 point after the high 5 is made. The next player begins performing the stacking pattern after receiving the high 5. The groups have 3 minutes to score as many points as possible.

Zippity-Doo-Daa-Daa!

Equipment:
- 1 set of Speed Stacks per group
- 1 cone

Directions: Divide the class into groups of 2-3. Station the groups around the perimeter of the playing area. Give each group one set of cups. In the middle of the playing area place a large cone (something the players may tag with their hands). Select one pattern for each minute of the game. For example, during the first minute the class performs the 3-3-3. During the second minute the class changes to the 6-6 stacking pattern. During the third minute, the pattern to be performed is the 3-6-3.

On "go," one player from each group performs the stacking pattern. After completing the pattern, the player runs and tags the cone in the middle of the playing area before returning to high 5 his/her partner (the next player). The group scores one point after the high 5 is made. The next player begins performing the stacking pattern after receiving the high 5. The groups have 3 minutes to score as many points as possible.

Note: The time limit may be changed and different patterns assigned to the different minutes.

Speed Wave

Directions: Position all of the players in a large circle. Each player has a set of cups. The goal is to find out how fast the group can complete a selected pattern – one player at a time!

As a class, select a stacking pattern (3-3-3 or 3-6-3 work best). Pick one player to start the stacking. On "go," the timer is started and stacking begins. As soon as the first player completes the pattern, the player to the right begins stacking. This continues around the circle with each player starting to stack when the player to the left has finished the pattern. When the circle is complete, the timer is stopped. Challenge the group to record a faster time and/or change direction of the "wave."

Criss Cross Speed Wave

Directions: Give all of the players a set of cups and have them sit in a large circle. Designate two players, who are sitting next to each other, as the starters. The group picks one pattern to complete.

On "go," the starters begin the stacking pattern. When the player on the right is finished, the player to his/her right begins the pattern. This continues counterclockwise around the circle. When the player on the left completes the pattern, the next player to his/her left begins. This continues clockwise around the circle. At one point the stacking will criss cross. The objective is to find out how fast the group can complete the pattern – one player at a time with the criss cross action.

Gold Medal Stacking

Equipment:
- 1 set of Speed Stacks per group
- 1 StackMat or stopwatch per group
- 1 scorecard per person

Background: This activity is great for an entire lesson, but may also be used as a warm up or to keep track of student progress. The idea is to set up levels of achievement for students to strive for while performing sport stacking patterns. The levels are based on time, with the gold level being the fastest time to achieve and the bronze level assigned, what might be called, a beginner time. Below is a table of suggested times for some sport stacking patterns.

Directions: Begin by grouping the students into 2s or 3s. Students within each group serve as judges for each other, making sure the patterns are performed correctly. Each student is given a scorecard (see next page) to keep track of his/her scores. After a short warm up period, students are given three chances, with the best score being recorded on the scorecard. The judge should initial each recorded score to verify the performance as being viewed and done correctly.

STACKING PATTERN	GOLD	SILVER	BRONZE
Individual 3-3-3	5.0 secs	8.0 secs	11.0 secs
Individual 3-6-3	7.0 secs	9.0 secs	12.0 secs
Individual Cycle	17.0 secs	20.0 secs	25.0 secs
Partner 3-3-3	6.0 secs	9.0 secs	12.0 secs
Partner 3-6-3	9.0 secs	10.0 secs	13.0 secs
Partner Cycle	20.0 secs	25.0 secs	30.0 secs
Upside Down 3-3-3	7.0 secs	10.0 secs	15.0 secs
Upside Down 3-6-3	9.0 secs	12.0 secs	17.0 secs
Upside Down Cycle	25.0 secs	32.0 secs	40.0 secs
Walking 3	12.0 secs	15.0 secs	20.0 secs
Shuffle	50.0 secs	1 min	1min 15 secs
Blindfold 3-3-3	7.0 secs	10.0 secs	25.0 secs

(continued next page)

SPORT STACKING
Gold Medal Checklist

STACKING PATTERN	GOLD	SILVER	BRONZE	Official Initials
Individual 3-3-3	5.0 secs	8.0 secs	11.0 secs	
SCORE:				
Individual 3-6-3	7.0 secs	9.0 secs	12.0 secs	
SCORE:				
Individual Cycle	17.0 secs	20.0 secs	25.0 secs	
SCORE:				
Walking 3	12.0 secs	15.0 secs	20.0 secs	
SCORE:				
Shuffle	50.0 secs	1 min	1:15 mins	
SCORE:				
Blindfold 3-3-3	7.0 secs	10.0 secs	25.0 secs	
SCORE:				

(Sample Worksheet)

CHAPTER FOUR

FITNESS GAMES & ACTIVITIES

Though sport stacking is not inherently fitness oriented, including sport stacking in a fitness unit can add a new twist! When incorporating sport stacking into fitness activities, students receive extra stacking practice while working to develop individual fitness! If stations are being used during a fitness lesson, try adding one or more stations with stacking!

AEROBIC CAPACITY

In order to increase aerobic capacity, a person must exercise for a minimum of 20 continuous minutes, 3 times a week, with the heart beating at 70-80 percent of the maximum heart rate. Most games will become stale to students after 5-10 minutes. However, if multiple games or tasks are used with minimal down time in between, the following games and activities will help develop and/or maintain aerobic capacity thresholds.

Ring My Bell Relay Challenge

Equipment:

- 1 set of Speed Stacks per group
- 1 desk bell per group
- Table (optional)

Directions: This activity may be done individually or with a partner. Give each individual/group a desk bell (or other device that makes a unique sound). Set up the playing area with a starting line at one end and a set of cups at the opposite end (20-30 feet apart). Determine which stacking pattern is to be performed. On the "go" signal, the player runs to the opposite end and performs a stacking pattern. Upon completing the pattern, the player runs back to the starting line and rings the bell. The same player continues for a set time limit (3-5 minutes). Set a goal for the number of "bells" within the time limit. Players may compete against each other or against the goals.

Note: The goals will vary, depending on distance traveled, time limit, and stacking pattern used.

Sample Goals:

5 bells = fast
10 bells = speedy
15 bells = super sonic

Jog n' Stack

Equipment:
- Speed Stacks sets as needed
- Index cards (stacking patterns)

Directions: Set up stations around a jogging track. At each station place a number of stacks and a sign designating the stacking pattern to be performed. The number of stations are determined by the size of the group. Generally the number of stacks should equal half the number of participants. To begin the session, split the group in half with one half starting at the stations and the other half starting with jogging. The students who are jogging first, scatter on the track. On the "go" signal, everyone begins. Joggers must complete three laps (the number of laps depends on the length of the track) before stopping at a station. While at a station, participants perform the stacking pattern three times before continuing with jogging.

This is a great activity to start class or as part of a multi-station aerobic workout. In either case, the jogging time should be 5-10 minutes in length. The stacking stations can be all the same pattern or all different patterns. Encourage the students to stop at all the stations. If a station is filled, students should complete another lap or move on to the next open station.

Challenges:
1. How many laps can each student complete within the time limit while stopping at a station after each lap?

2. How many stacks can be made within the time limit, while completing a lap between stations. For this challenge, designate one stacking pattern to be performed at every station. In addition, limit the number of stacks completed during each stop (1-3) with the students counting the number of stacks completed.

Jog n' Stack Aerobic Relay Run

Equipment: Speed Stacks sets as needed

Directions: This large group activity is designed for smaller groups of 2-4. Assign a number to each member of a group (i.e. number 1-4 if in groups of 4). Each group sets up a stacking station somewhere on the perimeter of the jogging track. Player #1 begins at the stacking station while the other members of the group line up, single file, on the jogging track.

On the "go" signal, the first player begins stacking and the players on the track begin jogging. The front player in the jogging line sets the pace as the group tries to stay in a single line. When the first player finishes the third stacking pattern, s/he runs to his/her group and joins the line at the back. The lead jogger runs to the stacking station and begins stacking. The new player in front sets the pace as the group continues to jog.

Variations:
- Change the time limit for longer or shorter jogging times.
- Allow the lead jogger to select the locomotor pattern.
- Change the stacking patterns.

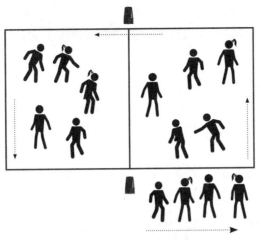

Double Trouble

Equipment:
- 2 sets of Speed Stacks
- 4 StackMats (optional)
- cones or tape (boundaries)

Directions: This activity is actually two games taking place simultaneously. Using cones or tape, make a centerline dividing the playing area into two sections. Create a stacking area (cups and mats) at each end of the centerline and out of bounds. In each section, a separate tag game is played. Designate a tagger for each game. If tagged, the tagged player crosses over to the other game and continues playing! However, before crossing over to the other game, players must perform a stacking pattern. Place a task card near the cups indicating which stacking pattern to perform before joining the next game. Switch taggers approximately every minute.

Variations:
- Create more tag games by dividing the playing area into four areas or quadrants. Place cups at each boundary line, connecting the different games.
- Designate a different stacking pattern for each entry area of the separate tag games.

Four Corner Sneaky Feet

Equipment:
- 2 sets of Speed Stacks (per game area)
- 5 hoops (per game area)

Directions: Set up a hoop in each corner of a 15'x15' playing area. Place another hoop with eight 3 stacks in the middle of the playing area. Assign one player to each corner hoop. The object of the game is to be the first player to make three 3 cup pyramids in his/her own hoop. One 3 stack may be taken from the middle or from neighboring hoops. Cups must be down stacked before taking them back to one's own hoop. Cups must be up stacked into a 3 cup pyramid before finding another stack of cups. Set up multiple games within the larger playing area. When a player has three 3 cup pyramids inside his/her hoop, the game is over and the group begins another game.

Variations:
- Upon completion of the game, winners must rotate to another game area.
- For larger cases (or smaller space), this game may be played in teams of 2-3. Teams use a relay format with only one player at a time from each group attempting to locate a stack of cups. The cups must be placed into a 3 cup pyramid before the next player may take a turn. Defending a hoop is not allowed.
- Use 6 cup pyramids instead of 3 cup pyramids.

Extinction Stacking

Equipment: Speed Stacks sets as needed

Directions: Establish a stacking area and divide your class into four teams. Everyone is a tagger. If a player is tagged by someone on another team, the tagged player runs to the stacking area. To rejoin the game, the player must complete a stacking pattern (teacher determined). If all the players from one team are stacking, the team becomes extinct and continues practicing stacking patterns until only one team is left standing.

Variations:
- Any stacking pattern will work in this game.
- For the shorter patterns (i.e. 3-3-3), designate a number of stacks that must be completed before rejoining the game (i.e. five 3-3-3 stacks must be completed).

Equestrian Jumpers

Equipment: 1 set of Speed Stacks per group

Directions: This activity does not focus on any of the stacking patterns but is a good warm up activity that uses the cups. Divide the class into groups of two. Give each group a set of cups.

Within the groups, students decide who will start as the "trainer" and who will be the "horse." Each group builds a hurdle using the cups. The hurdle may be a straight line of cups or built at different levels similar to a pyramid. The trainer and horse each test the hurdle by practicing jumping over it (bouncing, hopping, leaping as indicated by the teacher).

At the start of the game, the "trainer" sits next to the hurdle while the "horse" prepares to run. On "go," the horses run to any of the hurdles scattered around the playing area, trying to successfully jump each hurdle. The trainers reset their hurdle if it is knocked over. After 30 seconds to a minute, switch roles.

Save Me! Save Me!

Equipment: Speed Stacks sets as needed

Directions: Divide the playing area into four smaller areas. Assign two players to each area. One player in each area is assigned the job of "protector." S/he has the unheralded task of protecting the "dodger" (the other player) from being tagged. Separate the rest of the class, assigning them equally to the four areas. A line is formed at each area. The first person from each line runs into the area and attempts to tag the "dodger." The "protector" must complete a designated stacking pattern before the tagger tags the dodger. If the tagger is successful, s/he becomes the protector and the protector becomes the new dodger. The tagged player leaves the game and moves to a line at a new game. If the protector is successful at completing the stacking pattern before the dodger is tagged, the tagger must leave the game and get in line at a new game (area).

Variations: Select different patterns for each protector depending on his/her skill level. Faster stackers should do more complicated patterns (such as 3-6-3 or the Cycle) or perform multiple patterns (such as five sets of 3-3-3).

UPPER BODY MUSCULAR STRENGTH & MUSCULAR ENDURANCE

The following activities should be accomplished in sets. A set may be determined by time (1 minute, 3 minutes, etc...) or number of repetitions (10 stacks, 20 stacks, etc...). In order to help build muscular strength and endurance 3-5 sets are recommended.

3 Cup Pyramid Push Ups

Directions: Give each player a stack of 3 cups. While <u>remaining in an "up"</u> push up position, players try to record as many 3 cup pyramids as possible before losing push up form. Players use one hand to up stack and down stack switching to the opposite hand upon completion. Players alternate hands after every down stack.

3 Cup Pyramid Push Ups
(Alternating Hands)

Directions: Give each player a stack of 3 cups. While <u>remaining in an "up"</u> push up position, players try to record as many 3 cup pyramids as possible before losing push up form. Players alternate hands for every cup moved.

Ultimate Pyramid Push Ups

Directions: Give each player a stack of three cups. Players up stack and down stack while remaining in an "up" push up position. After down stacking, the player performs a push up. Upon returning to the up position, the player performs another up stack and down stack. The goal is to complete as many push ups AND stacking patterns as possible.

Flip Flop Stack

Equipment:
- 1 set of Speed Stacks per group
- 1 StackMat or stopwatch per group (optional)

Directions: A flip flop is done starting in the "up" push up position. While balancing on the same side foot and hand, the player turns until s/he is in the "crab position" or with the stomach facing up and balancing on the hands and feet. One more turn should bring the player back to the "up" push up position.

On the floor, place two stacks of cups approximately 4-5 feet apart. Starting in front of one of the stacks, the player positions him/herself in the "up" push up position. On the "go" signal, s/he stacks the cups up and down using alternating hands. After completing the first stack, s/he performs a "flip flop" to the next stack. After up stacking and down stacking the second stack, the player flip flops back to the first stack and restacks those cups. The player continues stacking and flip flopping for 1 minute.
This activity is best performed with a partner, with players switching every minute. Each player should complete 3-5 sets, stacking as many times as possible within the time limit.

Suggested Patterns: 3 stack, 6 stack

Log Roll Stacking

Equipment:
- 1 set of Speed Stacks per group
- 1 StackMat or stopwatch per group (optional)

Background: A log roll is a straight body sideways roll. Arms may be placed straight against the sides and legs or bent at the elbows with the arms tucked against the chest. As the player rolls, the legs remain straight and "stuck" together.

Directions: Set up the playing area with two stacks of cups set 8-10 feet apart. The player begins in the "up" position of a push up. On "go" the player begins performing the designated stacking pattern. Upon completing the down stack, the player performs a log roll to the next set of cups. When in the "up" position once again, the player performs the stacking pattern using the second stack of cups. Upon completion, the player rolls back to the first stack of cups. This continues for 2 minutes. Each player tries to complete as many stacks as possible in 2 minutes. Players should perform 3-5 sets of log rolls, alternating sets with one or two other partners.

Suggested Patterns: 3 stack, 6 stack

Monkey Roll Stacking

Equipment:
- 1 set of Speed Stacks per group
- 1 StackMat or stopwatch per group (optional)

Background: A monkey roll begins in the "up" push up position. The student lowers his/her body and performs a straight body roll (commonly referred to as a log roll) to one side. When the player is facing the floor again, s/he pushes the body back up into a push up position.

Directions: On the floor, place three stacks of cups approximately 4-5 feet apart. Starting in front of the first stack of cups, the player positions him/herself in the "up" push up position. On the "go" signal, s/he stacks the cups up and down using alternating hands. Upon completion, the player performs a monkey roll to the next stack of cups. Again the player stacks the cups up and down. The player then performs a monkey roll to the third stack of cups. Once the third stack is complete, the player performs a monkey roll back to the middle or second stack of cups. The player continues to stack the cups up and down followed by a monkey roll to the next stack of cups. The player continues for 1 minute.

This activity is best performed with a partner. The second player may serve as a timer and/or scorekeeper while the first player performs. Players switch roles after every minute. Each player should complete 3-5 sets of monkey rolls.

Suggested Patterns: 3-3-3, 3-6-3

Super Muscle Stack Shuffle

Equipment:
- 1 set of Speed Stacks per player
- 1 deck of playing cards per group
- 1 desk bell per group (optional)

Directions: This is a 2- or 3-player game. The players sit facing each other with their cups, a bell, and deck of cards (face down) between them. Assign an upper body exercise or activity to each of the playing card suits.

For example:

HEARTS = 3 Cup Pyramid Push Ups
CLUBS = Flip Flop Stack
DIAMONDS = Log Roll Stack
SPADES = Ultimate Pyramid Push Ups

The number on the card determines the number of repetitions the players must perform the corresponding task. The game begins with one player flipping a card off the top of the deck. One card is turned over at a time, alternating between the players. As the card is turned over, the players complete the activity.

Card values should be from 1-10. Eliminate the face cards or designate the value of a face card anywhere from 1 to 10.

Suggested Patterns: 3-3, 3-6-3, 6-6

ABDOMINAL STRENGTH, BALANCE & CORE STABILITY

Developing a strong core (muscles that stabilize the spine, pelvis and shoulders) is essential for functional fitness or fitness necessary for daily living and activity. A strong abdominal region and core help in reducing the stress of weight bearing and protect the lower back from injury. To maintain good posture and to help initiate powerful movements in the extremities, a strong core must be developed and maintained. As a result, balance, which is essential to all movement, is also developed. Below are activities that incorporate sport stacking into activities that help to develop balance and build a strong core.

The following activities require 1 Speed Stacks set per player, unless otherwise specified.

The Drinking Bird

Directions: This activity helps to develop balance and core stability while practicing the sport stacking patterns. The player places a 6 stack on the floor. While balancing on one leg, the player lifts one foot, bends at the waist and slightly at the knee while reaching down to the stack. The player builds a 6 cup pyramid up and then down. Upon completion of the stack, the player returns to an upright position <u>without letting the one foot touch the floor</u>. This is one repetition. Each player should attempt 5-6 repetitions before switching the balance leg. This activity should be performed for 2-3 sets on each leg. For beginners, substitute the 6 cup pyramid for the 3 cup pyramid.

V-Sit Stacking

Directions: This activity helps to build core stability and strength. It may be performed on the floor or on a balance disk. The player decides which stacking pattern will be performed (3 stack, 6 stack, 3-3-3, or 3-6-3 work best). The cups may be positioned between the legs or off to the side (player's choice). When ready, the player lifts his/her feet into the air, balancing on his/her buttocks. The player performs as many up stacks and down stacks as possible while balancing on just the buttocks.

Abdominal Twist Stacking

Directions: For this activity, which may be performed on the floor or on a balance disk, the player first decides which stacking pattern will be performed (3 stack, 6 stack, 3-3-3, or 3-6-3 work best). The player positions a stack of cups on either side of him/herself. When ready, the player lifts his/her feet into the air, balancing on his/her buttocks. The player performs an up stack on one side and then twists his/her body to perform an up stack on the opposite side. The player alternates side to side performing as many up stacks and down stacks as possible while balancing on just the buttocks.

Curl Up Stacking

Directions: Curl ups help build abdominal muscular strength and endurance. The player lies on his/her back with the bottoms of the feet flat on the ground, knees and feet together. Arms are crossed and hands placed touching the shoulders (never behind the head as this causes too much strain on the muscles of the neck). At the base of the feet, place a stack of cups. Set up the cups depending on which stacking pattern will be performed. Beginning in the "down" position, the player curls up and performs an up stack and a down stack, then returns to a down position. Give players 1 minute to perform as many curl ups as possible.

If done with a partner, have one player performing the curl ups with the other player counting. After 1 minute, switch roles. Continue switching until each player completes 3-5 sets of curl ups.

Lateral Shuttle Stack

Equipment:
- 2 sets of Speed Stacks per group
- 2 StackMats or 1 stopwatch per group
- 2 tables (optional)

Directions: This activity is best done in pairs. Place two sets of cups 8-10 feet apart. The cups may be on the floor but waist high works best (two tables). Player 1 stands in front of one stack and begins stacking on the "go" signal. After completing the first stack, player 1 laterally slides to the second stack. After stacking the second set of cups (up and down) player 1 slides back to the first stack. Player 1 continues stacking and sliding between the stacks until time is up. Player 2 is responsible for starting the timer and counting the number of stacks player 1 performs. After 1 minute, the players switch roles. Each player performs 3-5 sets. There are a number of ways to keep score for this activity:

(continued next page)

1. The number of stacks for each set may be added together for one large score.
2. Players may try to beat their own score for each set.
3. Players may compete against each other comparing scores after each set.

Suggested Patterns: 3 stack, 6 stack, 3-3-3, 3-6-3, 6-6, 1-10-1

Note: If the stacks are on the floor, do not allow the students to slide on their knees.

Class Lateral Shuttle Stack

Equipment:
- 2 sets of Speed Stacks per station
- 2 StackMats per station (optional)
- 2 tables per station (optional)

Directions: Divide the class into smaller groups of 2-3 players. Set up multiple stations (one for each group) around the playing area. Place two sets of cups spaced 8-10 feet apart at each station. Set a time limit for the entire class. Every team begins at the same time. Player 1 stands in front of one stack and begins stacking on the "go" signal. After completing the first stack, player 1 laterally slides to the second stack. After stacking the second set of cups (up and down) player 1 slides back to the first stack. Player 1 continues stacking and sliding between the stacks for 1 minute. Player 2 begins stacking for the second minute. Players rotate every minute for the length of the activity (10-12 minutes). Players record their scores after each minute. At the end of the activity, the groups tally their scores for a grand total.

Suggested Patterns: 3 stack, 6 stack, 3-3-3, 3-6-3, 6-6, 1-10-1

Jump The Cups

Equipment: Disposable paper or plastic cups are suggested here.

Directions: Though there is not any stacking involved with this activity, the cups are used to help develop coordination, balance and jumping ability. This is a partner activity. Each group is given a stack of 15 cups. There are three levels for each player to try and be successful. Level 1 is a row of five cups. Players attempt to jump over  the cups in a variety of ways. The jumps must be continuous with the goal being for a specific amount of time or number of jumps completed.

Upon successful completion, players may opt to move up a level. The second level is adding a second level of four cups on top of the five cups already in place. Level 3 is adding an additional three cups on top of the cups previously placed. Level 4 is to add two more cups on top of level 3. Finally, level 5 is to add one more cup to complete the pyramid.

Note: Cups may be knocked down and accidentally jumped upon, resulting in crushed and broken cups.

Variations:
- Challenge the players to use different jumping patterns (starting on two feet and landing on two feet, starting on one foot and landing on the same one foot, one foot to the opposite one foot, two feet to one foot, and/or one foot to two feet).
- Change the direction of the jumping patterns (forward, backward, side to side, forward and backward).

Forearm Balance Stack

Equipment: Stopwatch (optional)

Directions: Give each player a stack of three cups. Challenge players to complete as many 3 stacks as possible while holding a forearm balance. A forearm balance is performed while balancing on the forearms and the toes. The body is kept straight similar to the "up" of a push up except the player balances on the forearms instead of the hands. Players alternate hands for every cup moved.

Notes: This can be run as a timed event (30 seconds - 1 minute).

Suggested Patterns: 3 stack, 6 stack, 3-3-3

FLEXIBILITY

When performing static stretching, players should take great care in not over stretching the muscles which could result in muscle pulls or tears. Players should stretch just enough to feel a "pulling" in the muscle being stretched. Unlike timed events where the players are trying to complete as many stacking patterns as possible, the following activities are performed slowly with the main focus on stretching the muscles. Static stretching should be completed after a brief warm up such as light jogging. The secondary focus is on performing different stacking patterns.

V-Sit Stretch

Directions: Players sit on the floor with legs in a "V" position. At each foot, place a stack of cups. Players reach forward and perform a stacking pattern. The best stacking patterns to be used for this activity is the 6 stack and 10 stack. Players should perform 3-5 times for each leg. This activity helps to strengthen and stretch the hamstrings and lower back.

Figure 4 Stretch

Directions: Players sit on the floor with legs in a "figure 4" position (one leg straight, the opposite foot pulled up to the knee of the straight leg). At the foot of the straight leg, place a stack of cups. Players reach forward and perform a stacking pattern. The best stacking patterns to be used for this activity is the 6 stack and 10 stack. Players should perform 3-5 times for each leg. The adductor group of muscles and the hamstrings are strengthened and stretched using this activity.

Lunges

Directions: Lunges are used to stretch and strengthen the quadriceps, gluteal and hamstring muscles. Long lunges work the gluts more while shorter lunges work the quadriceps. Players start in a standing position for this stretch. When ready to begin, the player steps forward with one leg until the knee is at 90 degrees and above the toes. The rear leg becomes extended with the knee slightly bent. While in this position, the player performs a specific stacking pattern. One of the longer patterns such as the 10 stack, 3-6-3 or 1-10-1 is best to use. Players should perform the stretch 3-5 times on each leg.

Lateral Lunges

Directions: Place a set of cups on each side about one lunge away. Starting with the legs shoulder-width apart, the player steps 180 degrees to the side with one foot. The non-stepping leg completely extends. Keep both feet flat on the floor. After stepping to the side, the player performs a designated stacking pattern. The 10 stack, 3-6-3 or 1-10-1 are best to use. Repeat to the opposite side, switching legs. Players should perform 3-5 stretches on each leg. This stretch helps strengthen and stretch the gluts, hamstrings, quadriceps and groin (or adductor group).

Behind The Back Stack

Background: The idea to stack behind the back is a challenge in itself, but this activity is also great for stretching and actively engaging muscles in the upper body, specifically in the shoulders and chest.

Directions: There is nothing complicated to this activity. Players choose a stacking pattern, turn around so the back is to the cups and begin stacking. It is best to start with a 3 stack and work toward completing more complicated patterns.

A StackMat is optional if a player would like to see how fast this could be done. However, when speed becomes a factor, the focus will no longer be on stretching. To use a StackMat, the player faces the stack of cups with hands on the timer. When ready, the player turns his/her back (starting the timer) and after completing the stack, turns back and stops the timer. A partner with a stopwatch could also be used.

GENERAL WORKOUT

The use of stations is one way for students to work on developing different areas of personal fitness. The following activities may serve as a warm up (5-10 minutes) or as a complete work out session (30-40 minutes).

Fitness Stack Shuffle

Equipment:
- 1 set of Speed Stacks per player
- 1 deck of playing cards per group
- 1 desk bell per group (optional)

Directions: This is a 2- or 3-player game. The players sit facing each other with their cups, a bell, and deck of cards (face down) between them. Assign an exercise or fitness task to three of the suits. The SPADES are reserved for a designated stacking pattern.

For example:

HEARTS = Push ups
CLUBS = Jogging laps
DIAMONDS = Crunches
SPADES= 3-3-3 Stacking pattern

The number on the card determines the number of repetitions the players must perform the corresponding task. The game begins with one player flipping a card off the top of the deck. One is turned over at a time, alternating between the players. As the card is turned over the players complete the activity.

Notes: Card values should be from 1-10. Eliminate the face cards or designate the value of a face card anywhere from 1 to 10.

Suggested Patterns: 3-3-3, 3-6-3, 6-6, 1-10-1

Fitness Lanes

Directions: Create six parallel playing areas each approximately 10x40 feet. Assign an exercise or fitness activity to each "lane." Players pick a lane in which to start. On the "go" signal (music works great), the players begin to perform the activity assigned to the lane they are in. At the end of 1 minute, the players rotate to a new lane. Continue until the players have rotated through all of the lanes.

The FITNESS LANES may include any of the dynamic warm up activities popular at this time. Activities should focus on jumping, balancing, improving muscular strength and core stability. However, there are many stacking activities that may be included which would help develop individual fitness and also provide more stacking practice.

Suggested Stacking Activities:
- 3 Cup Pyramid Push Ups
- 3 Cup Pyramid Push Ups-alternating hands
- Ultimate Pyramid Push Ups
- Flip Flop Stack
- Log Roll Stack
- Monkey Roll Stack
- The Drinking Bird
- V-Sit Stacking
- Curl Up Stacking
- Jumping Cups

Fitness Ala Carte

Background: This activity gives students the responsibility for creating their own fitness stacking workouts by selecting an exercise and a sport stacking pattern. Designate 10-12 activity stations around the perimeter of the gym. Name each activity station according to the fitness stacking exercise assigned to each station.

Each player is given a set of Speed Stacks and a score card. On the teacher's signal, the players select a station, completes as many repetitions as possible and records their score on the card.

Sample Station Card:

THREE CUP PYRAMID PUSH UPS

Directions: Start with a 2-3 minute warm up jog. This is followed by a series of 3-5 minute workout periods. At the end of each workout period, the teacher will signal for the players to move to another station, giving students a chance to record scores before moving on to the next activity.

Fitness Ala Carte Menu

Name:		Date:	
Station			**Score**

Name:		Date:	
Station			**Score**

Name:		Date:	
Station			**Score**

Name:		Date:	
Station			**Score**

137

(Sample Score Card)

Fitness Station Rotation

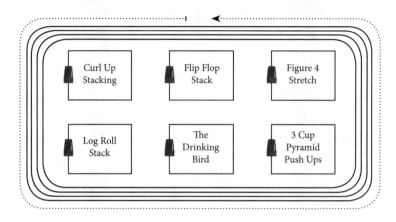

Equipment: 2 sets of Speed Stacks per station

Directions: This is a multi-station activity for which the goal is to complete all stations in the time allotted. Stations selected may focus on one or a variety of fitness areas. Students will jog for a specific amount of time while reporting to stations in between jogging times.

Establish a jogging track around the playing area. Within the jogging track set up sport stacking fitness stations, making sure to space the stations safely away from each other. Divide the class into 2-3 groups. The number of groups will be determined by the number of stations set up, as well as the number of students in the class. A class of 24 students, for example, may have three groups of eight students (groups A, B and C). With 5-6 stations set up, groups would take turns at each of the stations. Each station should be 2 minutes, giving the students time to complete the activities and record scores (if required). Groups B and C jog while the students of group A work at the stations. On a given signal, group B rotates to the stations while the rest of the class continues jogging. With a 2-minute station rotation, students would reach five stations in a 30-minute time limit while their jogging time would be 20 minutes.

Fitness Merry-Go-Round

Equipment: 5 sets of Speed Stacks per sport stacking station.

Directions: This is a multi-station activity for which the goal is to complete as many laps and visit as many stations as possible within a specific allotted amount of time. First, set up a jogging track. The track may be of any length, although this activity works better with an indoor or shorter track as opposed to a 400m outdoor track. Second, set up a variety of stations around the inside or outside of the track. Not every station will include sport stacking.

Three to four students should be able to visit each station at one time. The stations may address various fitness areas. However, if the allotted time is less than 20 minutes, it would be best to have all of the stations with the same fitness theme such as upper body strength. Finally, and this is optional, give each student a score card to record the number of laps completed and the stations visited during the exercise time.

Students begin jogging around the track. After completing two laps (as determined by the teacher), the students go to one of the stations. After completing the task at the station, the students would jog another two laps. Students continue to alternate between jogging two laps and completing each station. If a student has time to visit every station, have the student repeat his/her favorite stations until the exercise time limit has been reached.

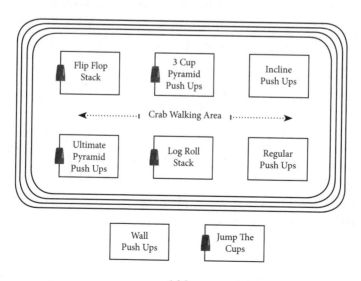

CHAPTER FIVE

KEEPING TRACK

In order to enhance improvement, students must be given clear expectations and goals. Setting up a system of keeping track of personal bests and rewarding achievement are excellent motivators in helping students develop better stacking skills and faster times. Below are examples of what a teacher can do to supplement sport stacking units.

Checklists

Checklists are a great way to keep track of personal best times. Personal checklists may be kept in a folder or portfolio until students are ready to practice or be tested. Time should be set aside during classes for students to try for a personal best while being judged by a peer or teacher.

Checklists may include any or all stacking patterns and activities the teacher feels is necessary to supplement the sport stacking unit. To keep track over the school years, lists may be divided by grade level or by age. Any list should include a level of proficiency for each skill or activity. The level of proficiency becomes the overriding goal for students to achieve. For the official competition stacking patterns and events, tournament qualifying times set by the World Sport Stacking Association (www.thewssa.com) are good to use as a mastery level of proficiency.

Rules for Testing:

1. Times only count when being watched by a qualified judge.
2. Judges are teachers or peers that the teacher feels confident are able to judge accurately and fairly.
3. Each student is given two warm ups and three attempts to set a personal best.
4. The best of the three attempts is the player's official time.

SPORT STACKING
1 Year Personal Best Checklist

Event	Mastery Time	Personal Best
3-3-3 Indiv. Stack	5 secs	
3-6-3 Indiv. Stack	7 secs	
Cycle Indiv. Stack	17 secs	
3-3-3 Partner Stack	6 secs	
3-6-3 Partner Stack	9 secs	
Cycle Partner Stack	20 secs	
3-3-3 Table Stack	50 secs	
3-6-3 Table Stack	1 min	
3-3-3 Mini Stacks	7 secs	
3-6-3 Mini Stacks	9 secs	
Cycle Mini Stacks	20 secs	
3-6-3 Upside Down	9 secs	
Cycle Upside Down	25 secs	
3-3-3 Blindfolded	7 secs	
3-6-3 Blindfolded	10 secs	

(Sample Worksheet)

SPORT STACKING
Multi-Year Personal Best Times

Activity	Master Time	AGE						
		6	7	8	9	10	11	12
Individual								
3-3-3	5 secs							
3-6-3	7 secs							
Cycle	17 secs							
Partner								
3-3-3	6 secs							
3-6-3	9 secs							
Cycle	20 secs							
Mini								
3-3-3	7 secs							
3-6-3	9 secs							
Cycle	20 secs							
Upside Down								
3-3-3	7 secs							
3-6-3	9 secs							
Cycle	25 secs							
Blindfolded								
3-3-3	7 secs							
3-6-3	10 secs							
Cycle	30 secs							
Relay								
3-3-3	1 min							
3-6-3	1:30 mins							
Cycle	2 mins							
Special								
Shuffle	50 secs							
Walking 3	12 secs							

(Sample Worksheet)

Wall Of Fame

Celebration of achievement is a great way to stir up enthusiasm and effort on the road toward accomplishing personal goals. The "Wall Of Fame" approach is simply posting the names of students who have mastered particular skills. The wall should contain a title card indicating the score one needs to have achieved mastery. A nice touch is to list the "school record" holder, giving high achieving students another goal for which to strive!

Collectible Cards

Collecting trading cards has been a very popular activity from many a childhood. Collecting baseball, football, basketball and hockey cards has become almost a national pastime! Trading cards are even found to include favorite cartoons, TV shows, and rock stars! Though more expensive than the checklists and Wall Of Fame ideas (cards for printing, ink costs), collectible cards are still great for rewarding kids upon reaching mastery of skills!

The traditional trading card size is 2-3/4" x 3-1/2". However, any size card can be used. The information listed on the card may be general or specific, bearing in mind the more specific the information is the more time it takes to set up and distribute. Below is a basic card that may be handed out as soon as a student reaches the mastery level.

3-3-3 MASTER

MASTERY TIME:
5 seconds or less!

MY FASTEST TIME IS:

_____

3-6-3 MASTER

MASTERY TIME:
7 seconds or less!

MY FASTEST TIME IS:

_____

THE CYCLE MASTER

MASTERY TIME:
17 seconds or less!

MY FASTEST TIME IS:

_____

3-3-3
PARTNER STACK
MASTER

MASTERY TIME:
6 seconds or less!

MY FASTEST TIME IS:

_____

(continued next page)

BLINDFOLDED 3-3-3 MASTER

MASTERY TIME:
7 seconds or less!

MY FASTEST TIME IS:

_____

BLINDFOLDED 3-6-3 MASTER

MASTERY TIME:
10 seconds or less!

MY FASTEST TIME IS:

_____

CYCLE PARTNER STACK MASTER

MASTERY TIME:
20 seconds or less!

MY FASTEST TIME IS:

_____

3-6-3 PARTNER STACK MASTER

MASTERY TIME:
9 seconds or less!

MY FASTEST TIME IS:

_____

UPSIDE DOWN 3-3-3 MASTER

MASTERY TIME:
7 seconds or less!

MY FASTEST TIME IS:

_____

UPSIDE DOWN 3-6-3 MASTER

MASTERY TIME:
9 seconds or less!

MY FASTEST TIME IS:

_____

UPSIDE DOWN CYCLE MASTER

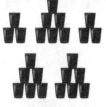

MASTERY TIME:
25 seconds or less!

MY FASTEST TIME IS:

_____

SHUFFLE MASTER

MASTERY TIME:
40 seconds or less!

MY FASTEST TIME IS:

_____

(continued next page)

ZEBRA STACK MASTER

MASTERY TIME:
50 seconds or less!

MY FASTEST TIME IS:

_____

SHORT STACK SHUFFLE MASTER

MASTERY TIME:
25 seconds or less!

MY FASTEST TIME IS:

_____

BLINDFOLDED CYCLE MASTER

MASTERY TIME:
30 seconds or less!

MY FASTEST TIME IS:

_____

WALKING 3 MASTER

MASTERY TIME:
12 seconds or less!

MY FASTEST TIME IS:

_____

CHAPTER SIX

USING CUPS IN NEW WAYS

Okay, so there are all these stacking cups hanging around. Is there anything else to do with the cups besides using them during a stacking unit? The answer is "Yes!" Following are some sample activities that go beyond sport stacking!

HELLO, MY NAME IS:

NEW!

Cup Catching

The sport stacking cups may be used in activities that help improve catching skills such as tracking and eye/hand coordination. Cup catching involves tossing or bouncing a ball and catching it with a cup. Any size ball that fits loosely inside the cup will work for cup catching activities. Balls that bounce and have some weight work best.

One Cup Activities:

Bounce and Catch: The student bounces the ball off the floor and attempts to catch the ball before it bounces again. Have students bounce with one hand and catch with the opposite. Encourage students to switch the bouncing and catching hands.

Basic Toss and Catch: Each student is given one cup and one ball. Students toss the ball up and try to catch the ball with the cup. Encourage the students to switch the hand used for catching. Higher level skills would include catching without letting the ball bounce off the ground and tossing the ball higher.

Partner Toss and Catch: Working with a partner, students toss the ball to his/her partner who attempts to catch the ball with the cup. Encourage students to switch the catching hand each time.

 (continued next page)

Partner 2 Ball Toss and Catch: Each student has a ball and a cup. Students toss the ball to a partner while attempting to catch the ball tossed to him/her by his/her partner.

Reaction Catching: This is a partner activity. Player A stands, facing away, approximately 8-10 feet from his/her partner (player B). Player A is the catcher. Player B bounces the ball toward player A. As the ball approaches, player B yells "turn" (or some other pre-arranged signal decided upon by each partner group). When the catcher hears the signal to turn, s/he turns, locates the ball and tries to catch it with the cup. The players switch roles. The ball may be bounced or tossed up in the air to the catcher. However, students should be reminded to avoid tossing/bouncing the ball directly toward the catcher's head, as s/he may not have time to react and catch the ball.

Partner Bounce and Catch: Partners face each other standing approximately 8-10 feet apart. On a signal, the players bounce the ball toward each other. The objective is for each player to catch the ball. If a partner group is successful three times in a row, each player takes a step back. Challenge the groups to find how far apart they can get and still be successful at catching. Variations would include switching the catching hand after each catch or reaching a set distance catching with one hand and then starting over while catching with the opposite hand.

Bounce and Catch Switcheroo: This is a partner activity. Partners stand facing each other, approximately 5 feet apart. On a signal, each player bounces the ball straight down and then steps to his/her partner's spot and attempts to catch his/her partner's ball. If each player catches the ball, the players take one step further apart and repeat the activity. For each successful try (both players must catch the ball) the players add another step back.

Cup To Cup: Each student has two cups and one ball. Challenge the students to toss the ball up with one cup and catch with the opposite cup.

2 Ball Cup To Cup: Using two cups, with a ball in each cup, challenge the students to toss the balls at the same time and catch each ball with the same cup.

2 Ball Crossover: Students toss the two balls up and attempt to catch the balls in the opposite cups.

Cup Passing

Cup passing is a rhythmic game played in many countries in a variety of ways. The traditional cup passing game objective is mainly to eliminate players by repeating a chant and rhythmic pattern involving a series of claps, touches and passing a cup faster and faster until someone makes a mistake. Whoever disrupts the pattern is eliminated and the remaining players begin again. Play continues until one player remains.

To create a more cooperative game (and one that may be used in a show or during a family night) have the players sit in a circle. Give each player a cup. Below is a sample of simple patterns to use along with some suggested songs. As the group becomes more comfortable, challenge the group with more complex patterns.

(continued next page)

One Cup Patterns:

Pattern 1:
- 2 slaps on the floor.
- 2 claps.
- Pick up the cup and place it in front of the player to the right.
- 2 claps.

Pattern 2:
- Pick up the cup and tap it twice on the floor.
- Clap 2 times.
- Pick up the cup and place it in front of the player to the right.
- Clap 2 times.

The Two Cup Pattern:

Give each player 2 cups!
- Tap the floor 2 times with a cup in each hand.
- Tap the bottoms of the cups together 2 times.
- Tap the floor 2 times with the cups.
- Transfer the cups one spot to the right and release the cups. (This is only one count and players should have moved one of their cups to the person next to them-the cup in the right hand should go to the player to the right and the cup in the left hand moves to the right hand.)
- Reach for the 2 cups. (8th count)

Suggested Music:
- "Rock This Party" by Rob Sinclair & Cutee B
- "Lollipop" by The Chordettes
- "The Hampster Dance Song" by Hampton and the Hampsters
- "Get Ready For This" by Crazy Frog

Additional Rhythmic Movements:
- Tap the bottoms of the cups with the player to either side.
- Leave the cups on the floor and tap the tops of the cups with the hands.
- Tap the open ends of the cups together.
- Cross arms while tapping the cups.
- Alternate the taps between the cups rather than tapping at the same time.

COOPERATIVE GAMES

The following games and activities are ideal for field days or family nights. More cooperative than competitive, each activity tends to generate bunches of laughter from the players involved.

Great Wall Of China

Equipment:
- Lots of Cups
- Measuring Device

Directions: The challenge for this activity is to build the longest wall possible using all of the available cups. Start by setting a minimum height requirement for the wall. Two or three feet is a good average height (this may be lower or higher depending on your group). To add to the challenge, give the players a time limit with the finished product being completed before time runs out. Measure the length of the wall and compare the results to other groups.

Pirate Treasure Chest
(Christine Walker, NJ)

Equipment:
- Lots of Cups
- Measuring Device
- Stopwatch

Directions: Players involved in this activity will have to put their math skills to use. Students are given the dimensions of a "treasure chest" found deep in the ocean depths. The task is to build a cargo box to transport the treasure chest. However, the cargo box size must be as close to the dimensions of the treasure chest as possible. Too small and the treasure chest cannot be placed inside the cargo box and consequently may not be transported. Too large and the cargo box will be unbalanced causing the treasure chest to dump its treasure back into the briny depths of the ocean.

Before the activity begins, create a treasure chest using a decorated cardboard box. Measure the box for its length, width and height (or have the players measure it, adding to the complexity of the task). The players must then figure out how many cups are needed to create a cargo box. Speed Stacks cups measure 3 inches at the open end, 2 inches at the closed end and are 3¾ inches tall (again, the measurements may be given or have the players do the measuring). After figuring out the final number of cups needed, the group sends one or two players over to a central area to retrieve the number of cups their group has decided is needed to complete the cargo box. The group builds its cargo box by stacking the cups. When finished (don't forget the bottom of the cargo box), the treasure chest should be able to fit snugly inside the cargo box.

Time each group to see how long it takes each group to finish the project. If the group underestimates the number of cups needed and must retrieve more cups OR overestimates and has too many cups, give a penalty time of 10 seconds per cup. Group times can be compared against each other or against an overall time limit.

Master Mind

Equipment: Cups of various colors

Directions: Divide the class into pairs. Give each player a stack of cups. Each stack contains six cups, each a different color. Partners must have exactly the same colored cups. Partner A sets up a pattern of three colors using the cups, without letting his/her partner see the pattern. Partner B must try to guess the pattern by calling out an order of colors. Partner A may not reveal the pattern but instead answers by telling how many colors are in correct order. For example, if the pattern is red-blue-yellow and Partner B guesses blue-red-yellow, Partner A would respond with "One is correct" (yellow). After which Partner B would guess another pattern. When Partner B guesses the correct order of cups, the roles are switched.

Note: Using more colors (starting with three) creates a more challenging problem. Encourage students to create a system of "guessing."

The Chicken Coop

Equipment:
- Lots of cups
- Measuring tape or yardstick
- Music: "The Chicken Dance"

Directions: The object is to build the highest and widest wall as possible. Place all of the cups on one side of the playing area. Designate a building area. Any version of the song "The Chicken Dance" may be used. Begin playing the song. During the verses of the song, the players build the wall. During the chorus, the players stop building and must perform the chicken dance. When the verse begins again, the players return to building the wall. Discuss different strategies for building the wall higher. Play the song as many times as deemed appropriate to the challenge (more plays will equal higher walls). This is also a great activity for a family fun night or cross grade levels with older students helping younger students!

Actions for "The Chicken Dance" chorus:
- Make "chicken beaks" with the hand open and close 4 times with the beat.
- Make wings by tucking hands under the armpits and flap 4 times with the beat
- Wiggle downwards for 4 beats.
- Stand and clap 4 times with the beat.

Mount Everest

Equipment:
- Lots of cups
- Measuring tape or yardstick

Directions: How high can a group build is the challenge for this activity. Using the available cups, players will have to judge how big a base to build and what type of design to use while still being able to go as high as possible. Give each group a time limit to complete the structure. At the end of the time limit, measure the height of the "mountain" from the floor to its highest "peak" (cup). Compare the heights and structure design between groups.

Rain Drops

Equipment:
- 1 cup per player
- Ping pong balls or plastic golf balls

Directions: The equipment needed for this activity includes ping pong balls and cups. Scatter all of the cups around the playing area, with the open ends up. A line is placed around the playing area. The task is to bounce the ping pong balls into the cups while staying behind the line. Challenge the group to decide on a strategy that will give them the most efficient and productive way of getting the most ping pong balls into the cups. The players may enter the cup area to retrieve balls not already in the cups. Give the group a set time limit. Discuss if the strategy used was the best solution or if other solutions might prove to be better. Have the group try again with any new modifications to their strategy. The name of this activity comes from the sound the ping pong balls make while the group is trying to bounce them into the cups.

Landing Site

Equipment:
- 1 cup per player
- Balls that bounce (baseball size or smaller)

Directions: Place all of the cups and balls (they must be able to bounce) in an area outside the playing area. The challenge is to create as many landing sites as possible inside the playing area. To create a landing site each player must take a cup and ball into the playing area. Each player attempts to bounce the ball and then place his/her cup on the ground trying to judge where the ball will come down! If the ball lands in the cup a landing site is established. The player leaves the cup (and ball) and returns to outside the area, retrieving another cup and ball to try again. After a set time limit, count the number of landing sites created.

Note: The ball must bounce above the head.

Group Juggling with Cups and Balls

Equipment:
- 1 cup per player
- Rubber or sponge balls (baseball size or smaller)

Directions: In groups of 5-7, the students must toss a ball to someone in the circle who is not standing next to him/her and who has yet to have someone toss a ball to him/her. Everyone in the circle should receive the ball once before someone receives it twice. Catches are made with a cup. Once a pattern is established, try to complete as many cycles through the group as possible without dropping the ball.

After the group figures out a pattern for passing around the group, add another ball! Add more balls as each group shows success in tossing and catching in the pattern. A discussion may be necessary regarding the use of bounces when more than one ball is being passed around.

Fire Brigade

Equipment:
- Large tubs of water
- Clear containers
- 1 cup per player
- Spot markers

Directions: A classic relay activity best played on hot, sweaty days! Divide the group into teams of 4-5. At one end of the playing area place a large tub of water. At the opposite end of the playing area place an empty container such as a pitcher or a clear plastic shoe box-size container for each team. Every player is given a cup. Space the players from each team an equal distance apart, approximately 5-10 feet apart (use cones or lines as markers), extending the length of the playing area.

 (continued next page)

On the "go" signal, the player closest to the water tub dips his/her cup in the water and runs to the next player. S/he then pours the water from his/her cup into the second player's cup. The second player runs to the third player and pours his/her water into player 3's cup. Meanwhile the first player remains on the second player's spot. This continues until the final player receives the water. S/he runs to the team's empty container and pours whatever water is in his/her cup into the container. Then the last player runs all the way back to the beginning, dips his/her cup into the water and runs to the next spot, starting the whole process of transferring the water all over again. After a set time limit, measure the amount of water collected in each container. Compare the results. (The teacher may choose to remind the players that the cups have holes in the bottom…or not.)

This activity may be made more cooperative by using one large common container at the end of the lines where all the teams pour the water. The final result may be weighed or measured in depth.

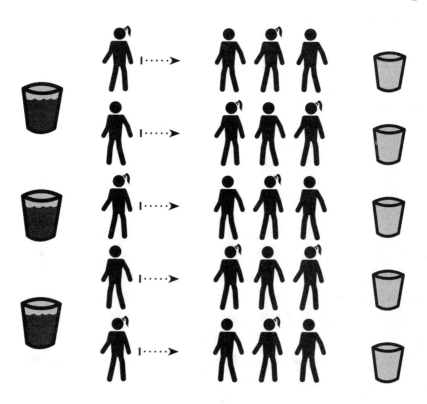

Water Toss
(Chip Candy, NJ)

Equipment:
- Large tubs of water
- Clear containers
- 1 cup per player
- Spot markers

Directions: The set up and playing area for "Water Toss" is the same as for "Fire Brigade" with the exception of the players being spaced 3-5 feet apart (instead of 5-10 feet). Players in "Water Toss" do not run to pass the water to the next player. Instead, a player must throw the water from his/her cup to the next player in line. Pouring the water is against the rules – the water must be tossed! The last player in line is responsible for dumping whatever water is left in his/her cup into the container at the end of the player area.

    This activity may be made more cooperative by using one large common container at the end of the lines where all the teams pour the water. The final result may be weighed or measured in depth.

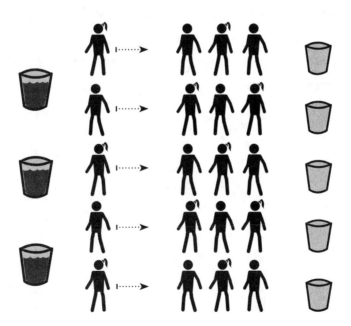

The Great Group Switcheroo Challenge

Equipment:
- 1 cup per player
- Balls that bounce (baseball size or smaller)

Directions: This cooperative activity works best with groups of 5-7 players aligned in a circle. Making larger groups simply makes the challenges harder to accomplish, though not impossible. Give each player a ball that bounces and a cup.

Group Challenges:
- How quickly can the group bounce and catch a ball? The task is complete when everyone has caught a ball.
- Can the group bounce and catch a ball simultaneously?
- How quickly can the group bounce the balls and catch another player's ball?
- How fast can the group bounce and catch a ball one player at a time?

Building Cities

Equipment:
- Sets of Speed Stacks (as many as possible)
- Hard surface
- Markers to define playing areas

Directions: A great field day game, "Building Cities" takes nerves of steel! This activity works well with groups up to 20-25. However, as the group gets larger, the number of cups needed for the activity also increases.

At one end of the playing area make a circle. Place as many sets of cups as possible inside the circle. Cups should be in stacks of 12. At the opposite end create a "construction zone" using markers. The task is to build as many towers as possible (see "The Ultimate Tower" on page 34) inside the construction zone within the given time limit.

The students within each group divide into pairs (2s or 3s). On the "go" signal, the pairs are sent to the circle in 5-second intervals (only at the start to help separate the group a bit). Each pair picks up one set of cups and runs together to a building area (a hard surface is needed). Once in the building area, the pairs begin to build towers. If a pair completes a tower, both partners run together to pick up another set of cups. Upon returning, the pair builds another tower. If a tower falls, the builders must stop what they are doing and repair the tower (watch out for windy days!). At the end of the time limit (5-10 minutes is suggested) count the number of completed towers.

Moon Craters

Equipment:
- 4 sets of Speed Stacks (each set a different color)
- Ping pong balls or plastic golf balls

Directions: Play this activity on a hard surface such as a wooden or tile floor. Create a 10-15 foot circle in the middle of the playing area (the middle circle of a basketball court works well for this activity). Surround the circle with a square. The lines of the square should be no closer than 3-4 feet from the circle.

Divide the class into four groups. Give each group a different colored set of cups. Scatter the cups (open end up) inside and around the circle. Assign each group one side of the square.

While staying behind the line, players try to fill the "craters on the moon" (cups) by bouncing ping pong balls (or plastic golf balls) into the cups.

Set a time limit (2-3 minutes) or continue until all of the balls are in the cups. Teams score a point for every ball that is in their corresponding cup.

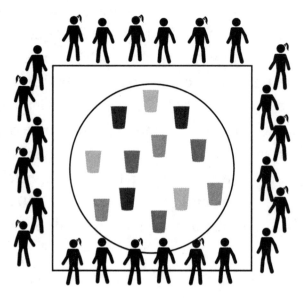

Black Holes

Equipment:
- 5 sets of Speed Stacks (each set a different color)
- Ping pong balls or plastic golf balls

Directions: Black Holes is very similar to Moon Craters, but has an added twist. This activity is played on a hard surface such as a wooden or tile floor. Create a 10-15 foot circle in the middle of the playing area (the middle circle of a basketball court works well for this activity). Surround the circle with a square. The lines of the square should be no closer than 3-4 feet from the circle.

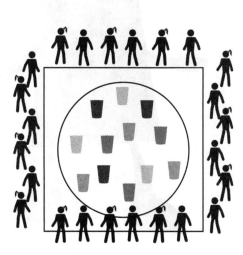

Divide the class into four groups. Give each group a different colored set of cups. Scatter the cups (open end up) inside and around the circle. Assign each group one side of the square. In addition to the team cups, scatter one or two more sets of cups in and around the team cups. The extra cups are "black holes."

While staying behind the line, players try to fill the "craters on the moon" (cups) by bouncing ping pong balls (or plastic golf balls) into the cups.

Set a time limit (2-3 minutes) or continue until all of the balls are in the cups. Teams score a point for every ball that is in their corresponding cup. Any ball landing inside a black hole is "sucked into the infinite void of intergalactic space." In other words, no team scores a point for a ball in any of the black holes.

SPECIAL THEME DAYS

Creating days with special themes provides a nice change of pace to practicing sport stacking patterns. Along with generating an abundance of excitement among the students, focus is still placed on completing the stacking patterns with speed and accuracy. Try inserting one or two theme days within a unit or make each day of the unit a different theme. Some suggested themes are listed below:

Doubles Day: Practice all patterns with a partner (one person is the right hand, the other is the left), activities are performed with a partner (or in groups of 2-3).

Team Building Day: Students participate in activities focusing on teamwork such as relays and cooperative games.

Special Stacks Day: Walking 3, blindfold stacking, and Shuffle Stack are examples of activities students would be participating in on this day.

Mini Stack Day: All patterns are performed using mini-stacks (available at Speed Stacks, Inc.)

Glow In The Dark Day: Turn the lights out and use "Glow-In-The-Dark" cups while performing the different stacking patterns. Glow-in-the-dark cups are available at Speed Stacks, Inc.

Relay Day: All relays, all day! Assign the students to groups of 3-4 and allow them to participate in a variety of relays. See "Large Group Games" or "Fitness Games and Activities" for ideas.

Fitness Day: Set up stations around the playing area. At each station the students stack while developing selected areas of personal fitness. See "Fitness Games and Activities" for suggested activities.

Stacking Circus: This is not a day of clowns and elephants! Set up the playing area with a variety of stations. Each station has a different stacking challenge such as balancing on one foot and stacking, blindfold stacking, and mini stacks. After a set amount of time, students rotate to the next station.

Combine Day: Assign students to groups of 3-4. Give each group a scorecard. The scorecard should have a list of activities (from basic to bizarre). Include spaces on the scorecard to record names and best times for each activity. After participating in an activity, students record their best times and then add the scores together for a combined team score. Recognition could be awarded to the fastest groups at each station based upon the combined scores.

Upside-Down Day: All patterns are performed with the open end of the cups facing up.

Potpourri Day: All patterns, all special stacks. Students have choices in which patterns to perform and what equipment to use (mini stacks, blindfolds, etc.).

Family Nights

Nights when parents and/or families are invited to participate in sport stacking activities are great opportunities to educate parents as to the benefits of sport stacking. The nights also serve as a comfortable environment for students to "strut their stuff" for their parents and siblings.

For the most part, the activities should be kept simple, as parents usually are true beginners when it comes to sport stacking. It is suggested that each night begin with "teaching stations." That is, set tables up where the students teach the parents the different patterns. It is also helpful to have the Speed Stacks instructional DVD on hand whenever possible for parents and students to view if there are questions.

The second part of the evening should be set aside for simple contests and games. It is suggested that the stacking patterns used be limited to the 3-3-3, 3-6-3 and 6-6. Besides recording individual times for regular stacking, other highly regarded activities include:

- Parent/Child Partner Stacking
- Blindfold Stacking
- Walking 3 (individual and relay formats)
- Topsy-Turvy
- Ring My Bell
- Tic Tac Toe
- Super Sport Stacking

The evening should end with a large group activity to bring the whole event together. Some suggested activities are:

- Chicken Dance Stacking
- Great Wall Of China
- Mount Everest
- The Chicken Coop

Family Night Score Card

3-3-3 Individual Stack			
Name:		Time	Time
Name:		Time	Time

3-6-3 Individual Stack			
Name:		Time	Time
Name:		Time	Time

6-6 Individual Stack			
Name:		Time	Time
Name:		Time	Time

3-3-3 Partner Stack			
Name:		Time	Time
Name:		Time	Time

3-3-3 Blindfold Stack			
Name:		Time	Time
Name:		Time	Time

3-3-3 Mini Stack			
Name:		Time	Time
Name:		Time	Time

3-6-3 Mini Stack			
Name:		Time	Time
Name:		Time	Time

Combined Times			
3-3-3	Name	Name	Total Time
3-6-3	Name	Name	Total Time

(Sample Score Card)

Teaching Tips

1. **Grip from the sides.** Teach players to grip the cups from the side, not the top. This will give players more control when releasing cups one at a time.

2. **Use a light grip.** Squeezing too hard will cause cups to stick together.

3. **Go slow.** When first learning techniques and/or patterns players should move at slower speeds. Learn the patterns first before attempting to speed up.

4. **Wait to use timers.** Learn the pattern first and then add the timer. The Speed Stacks StackMat is excellent for motivating students to increase their speed. However, when going faster students tend to sacrifice skill for speed, creating even more mistakes.

5. **Use different colored cups.** This is especially helpful with beginners. For example, when teaching the 6 cup pyramid, players can more easily identify where to grab the cups if the top three cups are a different color than the bottom three cups.

6. **Set goals.** Give the players a "master" time to achieve. This helps keep motivation and enthusiasm alive. Using the World Sport Stacking Association qualifying times is a good measure of mastery (www.thewssa.com).

7. **Repetition. Repetition. Repetition.** Players must build the "muscle memory" needed to develop a feel for where to grip the cups. This will transfer into faster times as players will not have to look at where to grip the cups.

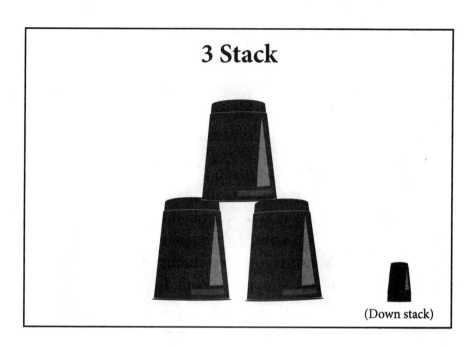

3 Stack

(Down stack)

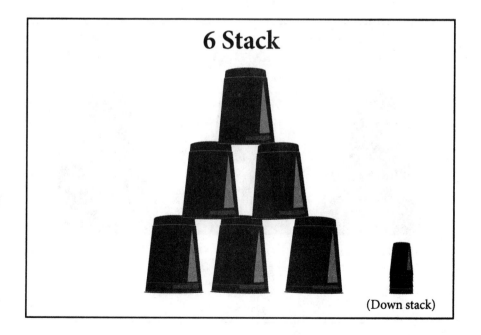

6 Stack

(Down stack)

(Reproducible Task Cards)

10 Stack

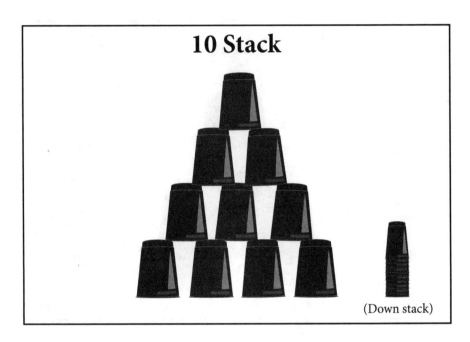

(Down stack)

3-3-3

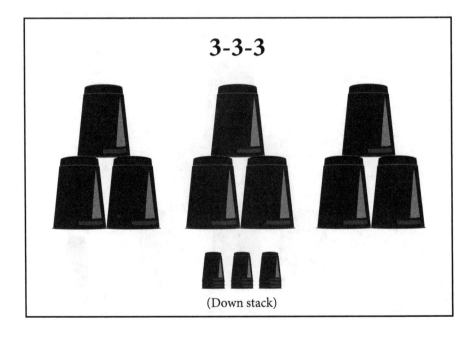

(Down stack)

3-6-3

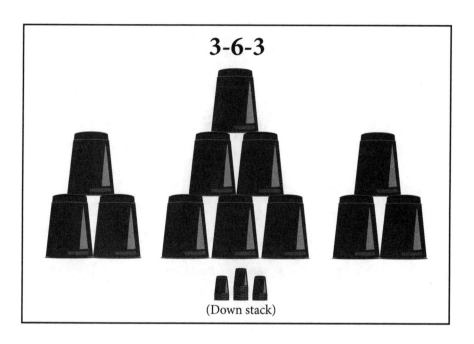

(Down stack)

6-6

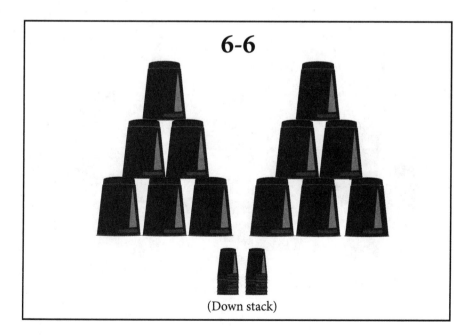

(Down stack)

(Reproducible Task Cards)

1-10-1

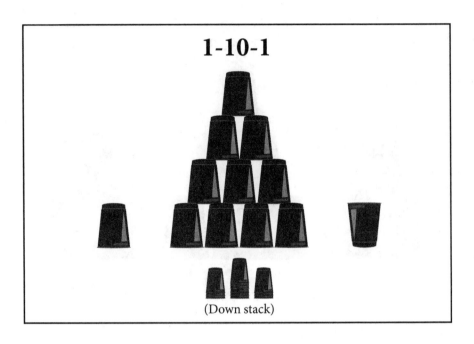

(Down stack)

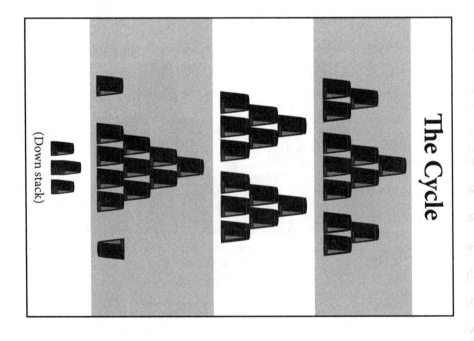

(Down stack)

The Cycle

GLOSSARY OF TERMS

3 Cup Pyramid: A pyramid with 2 cups forming a base and 1 cup on the peak.

6 Cup Pyramid: A pyramid with 3 cups forming a base, 2 cups on the second level and 1 cup on the peak.

10 Cup Pyramid: A 4-level pyramid with 4 cups forming a base, 3 cups on the second level, 2 cups on the third level, and 1 cup on the peak.

3-3-3: The simplest competition pattern. It consists of three 3 cup pyramids.

3-6-3: A 3-pyramid pattern using 12 cups. In order, build a 3-cup pyramid, 6-cup pyramid and another 3-cup pyramid. The 3-6-3 is a competition pattern as well as being part of the "Cycle."

6-6: Two 6-cup pyramids used in, but not limited to, the "Cycle."

1-10-1: Part of the "Cycle," a cup is placed on each side of a 10-cup pyramid. One cup is placed open end up and one is placed open end down.

Cycle: The premiere competition stack in sport stacking, consisting of three patterns: 3-6-3, 6-6, and 1-10-1.

Base Cup: When building a pyramid, the base cup is the cup left on the surface. It establishes the foundation of every pyramid.

Basic Grip: Hold the cups on their sides (not tops) loose and light. When holding multiple cups release them from the bottom of the stack one at a time.

Reverse Grip: Turn the hand so the thumb and index finger are on the bottom with the palm facing away from the body. This is used when down stacking the 1-10-1.

Speed Stacks: Specially designed high-tech plastic cups made for sport stacking. The official cups of The World Sport Stacking Association.

StackMat: Competition mat and timer by Speed Stacks. The official timing equipment of The World Sport Stacking Association. The optimum stacking surface with precision two-handed timer.

Set Of Cups: 12 cups makes a set.

Stack of Cups: Any number of cups other than 12 - usually three, six or 10.

Fumble: When cups fall individually or in a stack during up stacking or down stacking.

Up Stack: Building the pyramids.

Down Stack: Placing the cups in individual stacks/columns.

WSSA: The World Sport Stacking Association. This is the governing body for the sport. The WSSA sets stacking rules and regulations as well as oversees the administration of stacking tournaments. Website: www.thewssa.com

Sport Stacking Resources

Speed Stacks, Inc.

Speed Stacks, Inc. is the undisputed leader of sport stacking around the world. Founded by Bob & Jill Fox, Speed Stacks is the official sponsor and equipment supplier for the World Sport Stacking Association (WSSA) and all of its sanctioned and recognized events. It is here where the official cups and timing mats for sport stacking may be found. The family-owned company is located in Englewood, Colorado (USA). Anything and everything about Sport Stacking may be found on the Speed Stacks website at www.speedstacks.com. Visit their online store to purchase products (I highly recommend the Speed Stacks Sport Pack - it has everything you need to get a program started)or by calling direct 1-877-GOT-CUPS (468-2877). They offer grants, group order incentives and even loan out equipment!

World Sport Stacking Association (WSSA)

The WSSA promotes the standardization and advancement of sport stacking worldwide. Founded in 2001, the WSSA is the governing body for sport stacking rules and regulations and sanctions sport stacking competitions and records. In addition to tournaments and the World Championships, the WSSA hosts sport stacking's biggest event of the year every November in conjunction with Guinness World Records Day. The WSSA STACK UP! sets a new world record every year for "Most People Sport Stacking at Multiple Locations in One Day." It is a great way to get your students involved in setting a world record, stack up for local charities and often receive free equipment.

Go to www.thewssa.com for more information.